A Legally Created People

Dwayne Wong (Omowale)

CONTENTS

1 THE LEGAL CASE AGAINST REPARATIONS

Damages which are awarded in civil suits serve the purpose of making the party which was harmed "whole again." In essence, this means putting the party which brought the lawsuit in the position that he or she would have been in if not for the actions of the other party which caused the harm. In a personal injury suit where the negligence of one party has brought injury to another party, the guilty party may be made to pay damages for harming the innocent party. In this context, making the injured party whole may mean paying for the medical bills of a person who was severely injured and is unable to afford medical treatment or may be so severely injured that he or she is unable to work. In a contract dispute, making the injured party whole may involve enforcing specific performance of a contract which has been breached. This means that the court may order the party who breached the contract to perform the task which that party had promised to perform in the contract.

An important feature of the American judicial system is the idea of making an injured person whole again. This concept is important for understanding what the claims for reparations for African Americans are about. Reparations are about making African Americans whole again in the same way that civil suits are designed to make injured parties whole again. This is to be done through providing compensation for the collective damages that African Americans have suffered as a result of slavery and racial oppression. More so than this, however, making African Americans whole not only means compensation for the harms caused by racial discrimination, but also payment for the many years in which enslaved Africans were made to labor without payment. In other words, reparations are also about giving African Americans what is owed for centuries of unpaid labor.

Slavery was designed as a system in which one group profited through the exploitation of another group, but slavery was not merely an economic harm. Slavery was not merely the theft of African labor without compensation. Slavery also entailed physical, sexual, and emotional abuse. Enslaved Africans were subjected to being beaten, tortured, raped, and having their families torn apart. Slavery involved the intentional infliction of emotional distress. These abuses did not stop with slavery either.

In many respects the plight of African Americans is analogous to the struggles faced by Native Americans, who were also oppressed and dehumanized, yet there are some important differences in the two situations which have made Native American claims for compensation different. Native Americans have advantages in civil litigation for the recovery of compensation for past damages which African Americans do not have. This shall be addressed in more detail, but the point to be made here is that there are certain challenges which African Americans have faced in trying to bring civil suits that Native Americans have not had to confront.

In 1492, Christopher Columbus sailed to the Caribbean islands. In doing so, Columbus set in motion the European scramble to colonize the "New World." In reality, this world was only new to the Europeans who stumbled upon it. The indigenous people had been living in the Americas for a very long time and developed various civilizations, which were conquered by the European settlers over the span of several centuries.

This process of establishing European control over the "New World" was a very brutal one, which involved wiping out entire populations. In *Brief Account of the Destruction of the Indies*, Bartolome de las Casas documented some of the horrible abuses that were inflicted on the indigenous people of the Caribbean. This included being burned alive, sliced by swords, and devoured by hunting dogs. A queen named Hiquanama was, according to de las Casas' account, crucified. It is also worth noting that de las Casas also advocated that Africans be imported to labor in the New World.

The United States reflected the colonial reality of the Americas, in which the native people were violently dispossessed of their lands and in which - African people were imported from Africa to be utilized as slave labor. The American Revolution liberated the British colonies in North America from British rule, but the conquest of native land and the enslavement of African people continued much as it had during the days of colonial rule. In this regard, the treatment of Africans and Native Americans could be seen as a continuation of the colonial policies of England. The British Empire itself continued to enslave Africans in its own colonies until slavery was finally abolished in 1833.

The Seminole wars present an example of Africans and Native Americans working together to confront the oppressive conditions which they both endured. The First Seminole War lasted from 1817 until 1818. Representative Henry Baldwin wrote that the Georgia militiamen under Andrew Jackson "were, in fact suppressing an insurrection of slaves, aided by an Indian force, all assembled and armed for purposes hostile to the country." Baldwin's account gives the impression that the First Seminole War was a slave revolt which was encouraged and armed by Native Americans, although President James Monroe's administration attempted to depict the conflict as an Indian war rather than a slave rebellion. The Second Seminole War began in 1835 and lasted much longer than the previous conflict did.

The insurrection during the Second Seminole War was blamed on "mischievous Negroes and mulattoes living with the Indians some claiming to be free…and other fugitive slaves, runaways from citizens of Florida." Larry Eugene Rivers noted that the uprising did not produce a single outstanding leader such as Gabriel Prosser or Nat Turner. Apart from Abraham, whom Rivers refers to as the most important strategist of the rebellion, there were also leaders such as John Horse, John Caesar, Cudjoe, and King Philip. John Horse, in particular, had both African and Native American ancestry.

The relationship between America and Native Americans differed from that of enslaved Africans for two important reasons. Firstly, Africans were dragged from their homelands and brought to the "New World" to be enslaved. Native Americans, on the other hand, were already living in the Americas. Whereas Africans had to be forcibly moved from Africa to the Americas, the native population in America had to be forcibly moved from their own lands. Secondly, America treated Africans as property, but Native Americans were treated as nations. This meant that the American government could enter into treaties with Native American nations. In *Foster & Elam v. Neilson*, 27 U.S. 253 (1829), the Supreme Court held that: "Our Constitution declares a treaty to be the law of the land. It is consequently to be regarded in courts of justice as equivalent to an act of the legislature whenever it operates of itself, without the aid of any legislative provision." Despite the Supreme Court holding that treaties are the law of the land the United States was still willing to breach the treaties that were entered into with Native Americans.

In *United States v. Sioux Nation of Indians*, 448 U.S. 371 (1980), the Supreme Court held that the United States had not properly compensated the

Sioux people for the taking of their land in 1877. The case arose out of a breach of the Fort Laramie Treaty. In the Fort Laramie Treaty, the United States pledged that the Great Sioux Reservation, including the Black Hills, would be "set apart for the absolute and undisturbed use and occupation of the Indians herein named." In order to enforce this treaty, the government sometimes used military force to protect the land of the Sioux people from prospectors and settlers.

The executive branch of the government eventually decided to abandon the treaty. In a letter dated November 9, 1875, Lieutenant General Philip H. Sheridan reported that he had met with President Ulysses Grant, the Secretary of the Interior, and the Secretary of War, and that the President had decided that the military should make no further resistance to the occupation of the Black Hills by miners, "it being his belief that such resistance only increased their desire and complicated the troubles." These orders were to be enforced "quietly," and the President's decision was to remain "confidential." Without the army to enforce the Fort Laramie Treaty, there was a large influx of settlers into the Black Hills.

In 1877, Congress passed an act which abrogated the Fort Laramie Treaty. The Sioux regarded this as a breach of the treaty. After several years of lobbying, the Sioux were successful in obtaining from Congress a jurisdictional act which finally provided them a forum to adjudicate all of the claims against the United States regarding the treaty.

The Supreme Court in this case held that the Sioux people were entitled to just compensation for the taking of their land under the Just Compensation clause of the Fifth Amendment. The Sioux people were finally given justice, although it came more than a century after the injury had occurred.

The Sioux were compensated for an injury which they had suffered more than a century prior. It did not matter to the Supreme Court that the parties involved in the original injury were dead because there was an agreement in place between the Sioux Nation and the American government. No such agreements were in place between the American government and African people, however. The enslavement of African people was not the result of a treaty or a contract between the government and the enslaved, therefore nothing was owed to enslaved Africans.

The Supreme Court explained in *Foster & Elam v. Neilson* that a "treaty is in the nature of a contract between two nations, not a legislative act." Unlike Native Americans, Africans were stolen from their nations. Moreover, African Americans were stolen from nations which did not enter into treaties with the United States. African rulers did not go to the United States to draft treaties regarding the terms of the slave trade with the American government. The slave trade also continued in spite of numerous efforts on the part of the American government to outlaw the slave trade.

Some may argue the slave trade was an agreement between the European slave traders and the African monarchs who participated in the slave trade, but this would only appear so on its face. In reality, there was no equal partnership or equal trade. Europeans benefited much more than African nations did. It is true that African monarchs willingly participated in the slave trade, but this was not done on equal terms. When Afonso of the Kongo requested that the slave trade be brought to an end in his kingdom, his request went ignored by the Portuguese and some of the slave traders attempted to assassinate Afonso. The ruler of Benin initially refused to provide male captives to European slave traders given that male captives were typically incorporated into Benin's society. In the end, Benin's ruler was eventually persuaded to give in to the European demands. Rather than respecting the terms laid out by African rulers, Europeans employed various methods to impose their terms on reluctant or unwilling monarchs.

In order to acquire more captives to be employed as slave labor, Europeans would instigate conflicts among African nations or intervene in existing conflicts by supporting one side against the other. An example of this is the support that Nzinga received from the Dutch during her war against Portuguese slave traders. This meant that regardless of which side won in these conflicts, European slave traders profited from the conflict by acquiring captives. The slave trade was not conducted with any respect for the independence of African nations or respect for the rule of law in African societies. The slave trade, though profitable for Western nations, became a drain on African societies. Even those societies that participated in the slave trade were also adversely impacted by the trade as well.

It is important to note that in the scramble to conquer Native American territory, the United States had never ceased to view Native Americans as being nations. In *Johnson v. M'Intosh*, 21 U.S. (8 Wheat.) 543 (1823), the Supreme Court held that private citizens could not purchase lands from Native Americans. The court's ruling on this matter was consistent with the general lack of rights that were provided to the native people of the Americas. Chief Justice John Marshall wrote: "Conquest gives a title which the Courts of the conqueror cannot deny, whatever the private and speculative opinions of individuals may be, respecting the original justice of the claim which has been successfully asserted. The British government, which was then our government, and whose rights have passed to the United States, asserted a title to all the lands occupied by Indians, within the chartered limits of the British colonies. It asserted also a limited sovereignty over them, and the exclusive right of extinguishing the title which occupancy gave to them."

Chief Justice Marshall was clearly pointing out that America's policies towards the native population was a continuation of Britain's policy, which was a policy of territorial expansion at the expense of the native population. In his opinion, Chief Justice Marshall also established that Native Americans were no longer an independent people, explaining: "Even if it should be admitted that the Indians were originally an independent people, they have ceased to be so. A nation that has passed under the dominion of another, is no longer a sovereign state." What is important to note here is the fact that Native Americans were under the dominion of the European settlers. As such, Native Americans were treated as a dominated people, rather than being incorporated into America as equal citizens. Therefore, Native Americans held very limited rights under the American legal system, but Native American nations were still recognized as such, although they were not recognized as sovereign states.

Chief Justice Marshall concluded that conquest and domination of the native people were the only solution, explaining that "tribes of Indians inhabiting this country were fierce savages, whose occupation was war, and whose subsistence was drawn chiefly from the forest." Marshall also asked: "What was the inevitable consequence of this state of things?" His answer is that frequent "and bloody wars, in which the whites were not always the aggressors, unavoidably ensued. European policy, numbers, and skill prevailed. As the white population advanced, that of the Indians necessarily receded." Such statements by Marshall effectively upheld that land that was stolen through conquest was the legal property of the conqueror. Marshall claimed that the Supreme Court was not defending the way European nations took land by conquest, but he sought to justify the theft of land by conquest, nevertheless. Marshall declared that "we do not mean to engage in the defense of those principles which Europeans have applied to Indian title, they may, we think, find some excuse, if not justification, in the character and habits of the people whose rights have been wrested from them."

Less than a decade after the Supreme Court ruling in *Johnson v. M'Intosh*, President Andrew Jackson passed the Indian Removal Act, which led to the forced relocation of the Cherokee people. Thousands of Cherokee died along this brutal journey, which became known as the Trail of Tears. Marshall's ruling in *Johnson v. M'Intosh* helped to lay a foundation for the legality of Jackson's act by establishing that Native Americans were merely savages who could not be left in the possession of their own territory.

Johnson v. M'Intosh would not be the last time that Chief Justice Marshall would deliver an opinion on a case involving the rights of Native Americans. Chief Justice Marshall also wrote the opinion in *Cherokee Nation v. Georgia* 30 U.S. (5 Pet.) 1 (1831). In this case, the Cherokee people brought a motion for an injunction to prevent the execution of a Georgia law which would "go directly to annihilate the Cherokees as a political society, and to seize, for the use of Georgia, the lands of the nation which have been assured to them by the United States in solemn treaties repeatedly made and still in force." The Supreme Court in this case held that the Court did not have jurisdiction to hear the case. The Court held that the Cherokee Nation was neither a state nor a foreign nation.

Chief Justice Marshall stated very plainly: "The Indians are acknowledged to have an unquestionable, and heretofore an unquestioned right to the lands they occupy, until that right shall be extinguished by a voluntary cession to our government." In essence, the native population were under the control of the American government because, as Chief Justice Marshall pointed out, Native American nations were not viewed as being independent nations, but as "domestic dependent nations." Chief Justice Marshall also compared the relationship between Native Americans and the United States to "a ward to his guardian." Chief Justice Marshall even went so far as to infantilize Native Americans by explaining that they "look to our government for protection; rely upon its kindness and its power; appeal to it for relief to their wants; and address the president as their great father."

The problem with what Marshall stated is that the United States was not a kind and protective parent towards the native population. The Indian Removal Act clearly demonstrated this. Acts of violence and aggression which were aimed at seizing land from Native Americans continued, but what protection did Native Americans enjoy? How were Native Americans able to protect themselves from this aggression? Chief Justice Marshall made it clear that the Supreme Court was not an institution which Native Americans could look to for protection. He explained: "If it be true that the Cherokee nations have rights, this is not the tribunal in which those rights are to be asserted. If it be true that wrongs have been inflicted, and that still greater are to be apprehended, this is not the tribunal which can redress the past or prevent the future."

The Supreme Court would again affirm this lack of protection for Native Americans in *Tee-Hit-Ton Indians v. United States*, 348 U.S. 272 (1955). In this case, the Tlingit tribe, which is a subset of the Tee-Hit-Tons, brought an action for compensation under the Fifth Amendment of the Constitution. The Tlingit were seeking compensation for the timber which was taken from their land by the United States.

Justice Stanley Reed, who wrote the opinion for the Court, stated: "No case in this Court has ever held that taking of Indian title or use by Congress required compensation." The circumstances in which Native Americans were compensated for the loss of their land were circumstances in which there was a treaty in place which recognized the indigenous possession of the land, but there was no treaty involved in this particular case.

Justice Reed also explained that the position of Native Americans "has long been rationalized by the legal theory that discovery and conquest gave the conquerors sovereignty over and ownership of the lands thus obtained." The ruling in this case affirmed that Native Americans were a people who lost control of their lands due to conquest and that the American government could extinguish "Indian title" without providing compensation for doing so.

The petitioner in this case claimed that when Russia took Alaska, the Tlingit people had a well-developed social order which included the concept of property ownership and that when Russia possessed Alaska, Russia did not interfere with their claim to land. The American government, however, contended that the Tee-Hit-Ton merely maintained the right to use the land at the government's will and that Congress never recognized any legal interest of the petitioner in the land.

As noted previously, Native American nations have held a different legal position than enslaved African people. This is because Native Americans were viewed as nations—albeit dependent nations which were conquered by European settlers. Enslaved African people were not viewed as a collective nation. Enslaved Africans were property and as such had very little rights. For this reason, African people had a much different legal relationship with the American government than Native Americans had. It is necessary to understand this legal relationship between African people and the American government in order to understand the legal obstacles that stand in the way of legal suits to recover reparations for slavery.

First, it is necessary to understand the merits of a claim for reparations on behalf of the descendants of those who were enslaved. Slavery was abolished in the United States in 1865. This was followed by a period known as the Reconstruction, which was a period of tremendous social transformation for African Americans, which included several African Americans being elected into political positions. It was during this period that the first African American governor, mayor, senator, and representative were elected.

During the Reconstruction period, the Freedmen's Bureau was established by the government to assist the newly freed slaves. In *Souls of Black Folk*, W.E.B. Du Bois provided the following description of the government's policies during Reconstruction:

Thus did the United States government definitely assume charge of the emancipated Negro as the ward of the nation. It was a tremendous undertaking. Here at a stroke of the pen was erected a government of millions of men,—and not ordinary men either, but black men emasculated by a peculiarly complete system of slavery, centuries old; and now, suddenly, violently, they come into a new birthright, at a time of war and passion, in the midst of the stricken and embittered population of their former masters.

Reconstruction abruptly ended due to the Compromise of 1877, which gave the Republican Rutherford Hayes the White House in exchange for removing federal troops from the South. The removal of federal protection signaled the end of the Reconstruction policies and the beginning of a period of terror and repression. This was a period in which many of the gains which were made during the Reconstruction period were reversed and Jim Crow laws were implemented to restrict African Americans. Due to the civil rights movement these Jim Crow laws were overturned, but it is worth nothing that reparations were never paid for the damages caused during the period of segregation which followed the abolition of slavery. For example, no legislation was passed to compensate the family members of lynching victims.

It is also important to note that the Thirteenth Amendment abolished slavery, except under certain conditions. The amendment reads: "Neither slavery nor involuntary servitude, except as a punishment for crime whereof the party shall have been duly convicted, shall exist within the United States, or any place subject to their jurisdiction." In other words, slavery was still legal if done as a form of punishment for a crime. This clause was used to re-enslave African Americans. Vagrancy laws were imposed, so that any African American who failed to prove that he or she was employed could be arrested and imprisoned for vagrancy. African American prisoners were then leased to private entities to labor without pay. Prisoners were made to perform tasks such as picking cotton or working in coal mines which were owned by private companies. This labor was very brutal and there were instances in which men were worked to death in the mines. Women convicts were also put to work, usually doing domestic tasks such as washing and cooking. Some of these women were sexually exploited as well.

At no point after the abolition of slavery was there an attempt to compensate African Americans for the injuries which were suffered during slavery because these injuries continued. The end of slavery was not the end of racial oppression. One may argue that there were affirmative action programs which were implemented, but affirmative action was implemented to prevent future acts of discrimination, not to remedy prior acts of discrimination. Moreover, apart from the economic harm that has been inflicted on African Americans, there is also the issue of the psychological stress and trauma that has been suffered due to racial oppression. Take for example the trauma associated with lynching. Not only were black men unjustly executed in a very brutal manner, but no programs or policies were put in place to compensate the family members of those who were brutally lynched. African Americans experienced generations of emotional trauma, for which no compensation was ever provided.

The end of slavery in the United States did not bring about an end to the oppression and racial injustices that African people have endured. There was never an attempt made to repair the harm caused by slavery because the harms only persisted. For this reason, reparations should be understood as an attempt to repair the damage caused by centuries of racial oppression. It should be understood not merely as a monetary payment being made due to some abstract harm which was suffered by African Americans in the past, but as a means to make African Americans whole again.

Randall Robinson wrote a book titled *The Debt* which frames reparations as being a debt which America owes African Americans for years of unpaid labor and suffering. Robison writes that "black people worked long, hard, killing days, years, centuries—and they were never *paid.* The value of their labor went into others' pockets—plantation owners, northern entrepreneurs, state treasuries, the United States government." Malcolm X explained that the labor which enslaved Africans engaged in was an investment and that African Americans were seeking a return in that investment. Malcolm stated that "all we're doing there is trying to collect for our investment. Our mothers and fathers invested sweat and blood. Three hundred and ten years we worked in this country without a dime in return […]." Some have opted to use the judicial system as a means to collect on this debt or investment, but with no success.

Cato v. U.S., 70 F.3d 1103 (1995) involved a suit on the part of two groups of plaintiffs which included Jewel Cato and others. Cato sought $100,000,000 for "forced, ancestral indoctrination into a foreign society; kidnapping of ancestors from Africa; forced labor; breakup of families; removal of traditional values; deprivations of freedom; and imposition of oppression, intimidation, miseducation and lack of information about various aspects of their indigenous character." Cato was not seeking compensation for any particular harm which befell her, but rather compensation for racial injustices which had been committed in the past and which were never remedied. Cato also argued that these injustices constituted a continuing act since "African Americans continue to face virtually unfettered police activity and intolerance by others [...]."

The district court dismissed Cato's case, so it was brought before the Court of Appeals in the Ninth Circuit. Cato analogized her case to recent cases arising under the Indian Trade and Intercourse Act, such as *Oneida Indian Nation of New York v. State of N.Y.*, 691 F.2d 1070 (1982). The court was not persuaded by this analogy, explaining:

Analogy to Indian land claim cases is not persuasive, for the courts' willingness to hear the kind of claim exemplified by Oneida does not turn on whether the claims were based on a prohibition. Rather, Oneida, for example, turned on the well-established rule that a suit by the United States as trustee on behalf of an Indian Tribe is not subject to state delay-based defenses, and the anomalous result that would otherwise obtain if the trustee were allowed to sue under more favorable conditions than those afforded the tribes themselves.

The court further noted that "regardless of whether there are factual similarities between the treatment accorded Indian Tribes and African American slaves and their descendants (as Cato contends), there is nothing in the relationship between the United States and any other persons, including African American slaves and their descendants, that is legally comparable to the unique relationship between the United States and Indian Tribes. Courts have recognized fiduciary responsibilities running from the United States to Indian Tribes because of specific treaty obligations and a network of statutes that by their own terms impose specific duties on the government." There were no treaty obligations towards African people because African people in the United States were not viewed as being a separate nation.

The court in *Cato* noted that Cato's claim seemed to have been patterned after the reparations which was authorized by Congress for individuals of Japanese ancestry who were forced into internment camps during World War II. As the court in *Cato* noted, the reparations awarded to the Japanese was an act of Congress, not reparations which were won through a legal claim in court. Prior to the Civil Liberties Act of 1988, which provided Japanese Americans with reparations, Japanese Americans filed a lawsuit which was dismissed due to the statute of limitations. The reparations which the Japanese received was due to political legislation, not a court case.

In the case of *In re African-American Slave Descendants Litigation*, 304 F.Supp.2d 1027 (2004), a United States district court ruled on several suits which were brought by the descendants of formerly enslaved Africans. The plaintiffs were seeking monetary and injunctive relief against various corporate defendants. The court concluded that the plaintiffs did not have standing, which meant that they did not have a personal stake in the alleged dispute. The plaintiffs pointed to three injuries which conferred them standing to maintain their suit. The three injuries were being denied the wealth of their ancestors' labor, being injured on a continuous basis, and the plaintiffs argued that they "still endure daily indignities from the legacy of slavery, including, but not limited to, racial profiling, racial slurs, and improper and hurtful assumptions regarding their overall status." The plaintiffs also argued that they "are also likely to encounter future harm, as they are more likely to have a shorter life expectancy; more likely [to] go to jail; and are more likely to be murdered, than their white counterparts."

In order to establish standing in this case, the plaintiffs drew a direct link between the enslavement of their ancestors and the present struggles of African Americans, but the court held that plaintiffs "cannot establish a personal injury by merely identifying tort victims and alleging a genealogical relationship." The court also ruled that because the plaintiffs' alleged injury was derivative of an injury suffered over a century ago, the plaintiffs' alleged injury was "insufficient to establish standing, and contrary to centuries of well-settled legal principles requiring that a litigant demonstrate a personal stake in an alleged dispute." The court further stated:

> Plaintiffs' attempt to bring claims over a century old are barred by the statute of limitations. Plaintiffs have failed to assert any factual or legal basis for allowing them to proceed with their cause of action in light of when their claims accrued or with due diligence found that they would have accrued. Plaintiffs' attempt to avoid this legal reality by pleading vague factual generalities and chronicling the social and economic injustices that have befallen African Americans due to slavery.

The difference is that, as has been noted before, Native Americans were viewed as a nation and were therefore able to enter into treaties with the United States. That the treaties were later broken did not alter the fact that the treaties were signed and that treaties were the law of the land. The United States did not maintain any such agreements with enslaved Africans. Africans were not viewed as being an independent nation, nor were they viewed as citizens. The Supreme Court made this clear in *Dred Scott v. Sandford*, 60 U.S. (19 How.) 393 (1857). African Americans were also not respected as being a people who originally belonged to African nations, since the United States did not respect the sovereignty of African nations. As such, African Americans were a people without legal representation or legal protection. African Americans have historically occupied the space of not being fully treated as American citizens, but also not being recognized as a nation either.

It has been demonstrated that reparations for slavery and other injustices are not likely to be won through taking legal action given the task of having to overcome the statute of limitations and proving standing. Legislation seems to be the more effective manner of obtaining reparations for African Americans, yet legislation poses some challenges of its own. In 1989, John Conyers introduced the H.R. 40, Commission to Study Reparation Proposals for African Americans Act. Conyers spent nearly thirty years trying to get this bill passed and the H.R. 40 bill was not even a reparations bill, but a bill to initiate the study of reparations for African Americans.

Conyers pointed out that the impact of slavery was still being felt, explaining: "It is a fact that slavery flourished in the United States and constituted an immoral and inhumane deprivation of African slaves' lives, liberty and cultural heritage. As a result, millions of African Americans today continue to suffer great injustices." Conyers also viewed reparations as a world issue, which impacted countries outside of the United States, including African villages which were pilfered. Despite demonstrating the clear need for reparations to repair the damage done by centuries of slavery, Conyers also acknowledged that the proposed bill received much resistance as well.

The court in *Cato* rightfully pointed out that the reparations which the Japanese received was passed through legislation, not won through a civil suit in court. More so than this, however, the Japanese were compensated for a harm which was inflicted on specific individuals. The plaintiffs in *Cato* and *In re African-American Slave Descendants Litigation* were seeking compensation for collective harms which began during slavery and continued after slavery was abolished. The individuals who suffered these harms were not specifically identified. The court in *In re African-American Slave Descendants Litigation* ruled that the plaintiffs did not have standing because they were never enslaved. The court in *Cato* adopted similar reasoning. Cato herself was never enslaved, so the court ruled: "Without a concrete, personal injury that is not abstract and that is fairly traceable to the government conduct that she challenges as unconstitutional, Cato lacks standing."

One of the conceptual challenges of a legal case for reparations for slavery is that, as Alfred L. Brophy explained, "the victims are making claims against people who are not themselves wrongdoers." That is to say that the claims for reparations are made against individuals who did not own slaves, though in many instances it is easy to demonstrate that certain institutions did profit from slavery. Brophy further explained: "It seems that few deny that there are connections between past wrongdoing and present harm (though recognition of that fact may be more prevalent among victims than descendants of perpetrators), but the problem becomes putting that connection into some framework that law recognizes."

In the 1973 book *The Case for Black Reparations*, Boris Bittker made the case that federal and state governments were legally liable for more recent racial crimes. Bittker, who was making a legal claim for redress, conceded that reparations for slavery was unlikely due to legal barriers, but held the view that the law should provide a remedy for more recent racial injustices, such as school segregation. Rhonda Magee argued that abandoning claims for slavery reparations, though pragmatic, "eliminates the most compelling basis for claims and damages."

We turn again to Native Americans, who have been able to prevail in court over claims based on past injustices because of the existence of legally binding treaties which were broken by the party against whom the suit was brought. Yet it should also be noted that despite being able to prevail in claims regarding broken treaties, Native Americans have never been truly made whole because the land and resources which were stolen have not been returned. The previously mentioned cases demonstrate that the Supreme Court has repeatedly affirmed that Native Americans do not have absolute rights to their lands and that their lands can be legally taken so long as Native Americans are properly compensated for the taking of their lands.

If Native Americans, who were able to enter into legally binding treaties with the United States, have not been made whole again, then what legal arguments do African Americans have for reparations? Based on the two cases examined previously, there is no legal precedent for reparations for slavery within the American judicial system.

Even in circumstances where a court has ruled that the United States is at fault and orders the United States to pay reparations, the United States has refused. This was demonstrated when Nicaragua brought a suit against the United States regarding the United States' support of violent rebel groups in Nicaragua. In 1986, the International Court of Justice held that the United States violated the fundamental norms of international law and ordered the United States to pay reparations to Nicaragua. The American government decided to ignore the Court's judgement, however.

The case with Nicaragua further demonstrates the legal challenges associated with obtaining reparations for African Americans who have been victimized by racism because even in the field of international law, the United States cannot be compelled to pay reparations even if an international body such as the International Court of Justice rules that the United States is in violation of the law.

There appears to be very little precedent to support any successful legal claims for reparations for African Americans, but this does not invalidate the claims for reparations. In a 1993 article, Vincene Verdun established the case for reparations as a political issue rather than a legal one. Verdun left no room for distinguishing between harms caused by the government and harms caused by private discrimination because in Verdun's view American society as a whole is liable for the harms caused by centuries of slavery and decades of Jim Crow. Verdun views racism as both an economic and emotional injury.

American courts themselves have affirmed that reparations for slavery is a political issue, not a legal one. There have been certain non-legal arguments put forward against reparations which shall be briefly addressed here before we move to the conclusion. The first of which is that the United States was not responsible for slavery since slavery was practiced by the British colonial government prior to America's independence. This is true. In fact, the Dutch, Spanish, and French also enslaved African people in the various North American territories which they controlled. Based on these facts, a case could perhaps be made that those European nations which were involved would also owe African Americans reparations as well.

During the colonial period, some of the European settlers in the American colonies had in fact blamed England for slavery in the United States, but these settlers freely engaged in slavery and made little effort to put an end to slavery once they became independent from British rule. In a speech titled "Address to the Slaves of the U.S." the noted abolitionist Henry Highland Garnet highlighted the fact that the colonists in America blamed Britain for slavery in the colonies, but once independence came the United States did not immediately abolish slavery. Garnet declared: "The colonists threw the blame upon England. They said that the mother country entailed the evil upon them, and that they would rid themselves of it if they could. The world thought they were sincere, and the philanthropic pitied them. But time soon tested their sincerity. In a few years, the colonists grew strong and severed themselves from the British Government. Their Independence was declared, and they took their station among the sovereign powers of the earth. The declaration was a glorious document. Sages admired it, and the patriotic of every nation reverenced the Godlike sentiments which it contained. When the power of Government returned to their hands, did they emancipate the slaves? No; they rather added new links to our chains."

The African role in the slave trade has also been used in an attempt to obfuscate the discussion on reparations. In "Ending the Slavery Blame-Game," Henry Louis Gates raised the question of the African complicity in the slave trade for this purpose. It is true that there were African monarchs who participated in the slave trade, but those kingdoms which were involved were also victimized by the slave trade as well. Therefore, if one is to maintain that the nation of Benin, for example, should be liable to African Americans for the role that the kingdom of Dahomey played in selling captives into slavery, could not one also hold that Benin should also be compensated for the fact that many of the people of Dahomey were also kidnapped and sold into slavery? The same is true of the Asante Kingdom or of any other African kingdom which was involved in the slave trade. In the end, one is left to conclude that the slave trade may have been a benefit to some of the African rulers and some African slave traders, but it was also a great harm to Africa as well since it involved the kidnapping of millions, as well as the destruction of villages and even entire kingdoms. Europe, on the other hand, did not suffer the same devastation that Africa experienced. The slave trade caused a stagnation in Africa's development, whereas Western society developed an international capitalist economy from the slave trade.

Yet another argument which attempts to obfuscate the discourse on reparations is the argument that much of the debt owed to African Americans was paid by the Civil War, which was a very bloody and costly war which resulted in the freeing of enslaved Africans. David Horowitz argued that the Civil War was a cancelation of the debt. The war was not undertaken for the purpose of fixing the problem of racial inequality, however. It was mentioned earlier that certain steps were taken during the Reconstruction period to improve the conditions of African people in the United States, but this did not last very long and was followed by a period in which racist policies were implemented to keep African Americans oppressed.

The end of slavery was not the end of racial inequality or the end of the exploitation of African Americans, which is why reparations demands are often framed in terms of a continuous harm, as opposed to reparations for slavery alone. The abuses and the harms did not end when slavery was abolished. Critics of the demand for reparations deliberately ignore the element of racial oppression and economic exploitation, and merely reduce the discourse on reparations as being reparations for slavery. This is what Horowitz does.

Horowitz explains: "Slavery existed for

thousands of years before the Atlantic slave trade was born, and in all societies. But in the thousand years of its existence, there never was an anti-slavery movement until white Christians—Englishmen and Americans—created one. If not for the anti-slavery attitudes and military power of white Englishmen and Americans, the slave trade would not have been brought to an end. If not for the sacrifices of white soldiers and a white American president who gave his life to sign the Emancipation Proclamation, blacks in America would still be slaves." Horowitz's argument is flawed in that it denies enslaved Africans agency in their own struggle to liberate themselves from the "white Christians" who enslaved them. This is not to deny that there were white people who were involved, but the struggle to end slavery was a struggle primarily waged by African people.

Horowitz seems to want to ignore the fact that the white people who did oppose slavery and created an anti-slavery movement did so in opposition to how other white people were enslaving African people. In other words, it was white Christian slave owners who created the conditions which made an anti-slavery movement necessary. That it took a war to finally bring an end to slavery in the United States only demonstrates how firmly entrenched slavery was in the United States. Moreover, Horowitz neglects to mention that slavery was never outright abolished in the United States. The provision in the Thirteenth Amendment which allowed slavery to continue was addressed previously and shall not be recounted again here.

Horowitz asks: "Where is the gratitude of black

America and its leaders for those gifts?" Which gifts is he referring to? African Americans had to struggle to end slavery and to end Jim Crow laws. Freedom was not a gift that was merely handed to African Americans. It was something that some lost their lives struggling for. As explained before, Horowitz's version of history is one which robs African Americans of agency. Were civil rights a gift which was bestowed upon African Americans, or did individuals have to march and go to jail in order for the United States to pass civil rights laws which outlawed segregation? Was Harriet Tubman gifted with freedom, or did she have to run away in order to be free?

The demand for reparations has continued to persist for as long as it has because the United States has yet to fully make African Americans whole again and many of those who continue to suffer from the impact of racism seek a comprehensive solution which will truly correct the injuries of the past, as well as those of the present.

Selected References:

Alfred L. Brophy, "Some Conceptual And Legal Problems in Reparations For Slavery," *NYU Annual Survey of American Law*, Vol. 58, 2003.

Henry Louis Gates, "Ending the Slavery Blame-Game," *New York Times*, April 22, 2010.

James P. Rowles, "*Nicaragua versus the United States*: Issues of Law and Policy," *The International*

Lawyer, Vol. 20, NO. 4, 1986.

Larry E. Rivers, *Rebels and Runaways*, (University of Illinois Press, 20102).

Malcolm X, *Malcolm X Speaks*, (Grove Press, 1965).

"Representative John Conyers and the Commission to Study Reparation Proposals for African Americans Act," *Africology: The Journal of Pan African Studies*. 9, no. 5, August 2016.

2 BREAKING THE LAW TO CHANGE THE LAW

"A black man can't get justice in court. A black man can't get justice in the court system of America. [...] The only way you get justice is when you make justice for yourself."
-Malcolm X

In 1952, Nelson Mandela opened his own law firm. He eventually opened a firm together with Oliver Tambo. Mandela and Tambo were the only firm of African lawyers, so, as Mandela explained in his autobiography *Long Walk to Freedom*, the two were "besieged" with clients. Mandela explained that their firm was the first choice and last resort of their numerous clients, who were in desperate need of legal help. Mandela and Tambo were in court very frequently. Mandela explained that he and Tambo frequently dealt with prejudice in the court. White witnesses often refused to answer questions from a black attorney and rather than citing such witnesses for contempt of court, the magistrate would pose the questions to the witnesses that the witnesses refused to answer from Mandela. Mandela concluded that working as a "lawyer in South Africa meant operating under a debased system of justice, a code of law that did not enshrine equality but its opposite."

Anton Lembede, who was also a lawyer and a member of the African National Congress (A.N.C.), faced similar challenges in the courtroom. On one occasion, Lembede arrived in court and informed the prosecutor that he was the attorney of record. The prosecutor brushed Lembede off. Lembede responded by sitting in the public gallery. When the case was called, Lembede got up and announced from the gallery that he was appearing to defend the accused. This incident created a stir in the courtroom and it also demonstrated the type of disrespect which African lawyers in South Africa received.

Mandela, as well as other members of the A.N.C., came to the realization that there was no way to work within that debased system to create change, so Mandela and others turned to subversive and illegal activities to fight for change in South Africa. Mandela ended up serving twenty-seven years in prison for his activities. Mandela was one of several activists in South Africa that were imprisoned for resisting against apartheid. Mandela was a lawyer who was trained to understand the laws of South Africa and to operate within a racist legal system which oppressed African people. Ultimately, however, it was impossible for Mandela to produce any substantive change in South Africa by trying to work within the system itself, particularly within a judicial system which criminalized being an African. For this reason, Mandela and others were forced to engage in illegal activities to struggle against the unjust laws in South Africa. It was these illegal activities which forced a change in the racist laws of South African society.

The example of South Africa is mentioned to demonstrate the challenges of trying to change a racist system while working within the system itself. Often, it has been the case that the work required to create change within the system had to be done outside of the system and outside of the legal parameters set up by the system. In other words, those who affected change within an unjust society were lawbreakers because such individuals broke what they considered to be unjust laws.

In an unjust system, the people who are responsible for implementing and enforcing unjust laws often make it impossible for the oppressed to alter those very laws through legal means. For example, a brutal and oppressive dictator may rig elections to ensure that there is no means by which the population can remove that dictator electorally. In such cases, the population has to resort to measures which are banned by the dictator, such as massive protests or in some instances armed insurrection. In effect, the dictator makes it impossible for him to be removed in a manner which would be legal under the laws of the society which the dictator himself has constructed and in doing so the dictator is then able to legitimize his rule by criminalizing those who opposed him.

A Legally Created People

One particular example of this is in Togo, where Gnassingbé Eyadéma came to power through a military coup. He then spent the next several decades maintaining himself in power through the use of brutal force, which included torturing and murdering political opponents and activists. When Eyadéma died, the military once again seized power and installed his son Faure Gnassingbé as president.

Under the Gnassingbé dictatorship in Togo there has never been a "legal" way to protest against the dictatorship because any act against the dictator—whether it be an act of forceful rebellion or nonviolent civil disobedience—can be punished with force. Without the ability to vote the Gnassingbé dictatorship out of power, the only means available to the people of Togo has been to fight for change through means which have not been sanctioned by the regime.

The condition in the United States is not as extreme as the conditions found within military dictatorships, yet the oppression that African people have endured in the United States has been no less brutal and vicious. The United States is a nation where racism has been codified into law. Codifying racism into law not only made racial discrimination legal, but it also allowed the society to criminalize those who dared to stand up against such unjust laws. Much as dictators maintain their population in a state of terror and intimidation, African Americans were maintained in a state of terror and intimidation. Those who dared to resist were often punished because such acts of resistance were a violation of America's racist laws.

The United States is not a dictatorship. The United States has been, since its founding, a representative democracy where the president is elected for a term which lasts four years. The Twenty-Second Amendment was implemented to place a two-term limit on the presidency, further limiting the influence of the president in contrast to dictatorships where a single individual is free to reign for life, as Gnassingbé Eyadéma did in Togo. Apart from electing the president, who is the leader of the executive branch of the country, American citizens also vote to elect senators and representatives who make up the Congress, which is the legislative branch of the government. As mandated by the Constitution, senators serve a six-year term before their seat is up for election and representatives serve a two-year term. Finally, there is the judicial branch of the federal government which is made up of justices who are appointed by the president, with the approval of the Senate.

The ability to vote and elect representatives theoretically gives the average American citizen the ability to have a say in the governance of the country, but the reality is that when the United States was founded there were entire segments of the population who were unable to vote. How then could a group of people who were shut out of the political process affect political change in a representative democracy? The struggle for women's suffrage offers an answer to this question.

The Nineteenth Amendment gave women the right to vote. Prior to the passage of this amendment, women in America could not vote. Obviously, women did not vote in order to get the right to vote. It took mobilization and agitation on the part of the advocates of women's suffrage to get the law changed so that women were able to vote. The struggle for women's suffrage demonstrates that significant change in the United States rarely comes within the very legal or political system which created and perpetuates the condition which needs to be changed. Change is often the result of pressure being placed on the system by forces who are operating outside of the system. Nowhere is this truer than the struggles of people of African descent.

Apartheid was already noted as one example in which African people had to struggle for change within an unjust system by putting pressure on that system, even if it meant taking up arms and breaking the laws of the unjust society. Africans who were oppressed by American racism also had to struggle for change, which meant breaking the laws of the unjust society. This at times meant violent rebellion and resistance, or nonviolent civil disobedience. The illegality of the methods of resistance was not based on whether or not the resistance was violent, however, and this is important to keep in mind. Resistance towards unjust laws on the part of Africans in the United States was illegal simply because those who resisted opposed the law. It did not matter whether that resistance involved organizing slaves to rise up to kill the slave masters or if it meant refusing to give up one's seat on a bus. Any action which opposed the law was illegal and therefore those who offered resistance were criminals under the law.

An example of how resistance on the part of African Americans was punished was the fact that those who refused to serve in America's wars once drafted were often punished. Muhammad Ali was sentenced to prison for refusing to go to Vietnam to support the violent war which was being waged against the Vietnamese people. There were some who managed to avoid going to war through utilizing legal methods, however. H. Rap Brown was drafted for military service. Rather than outright refusing to serve, Brown went to the army base where he caused such a commotion that he was rejected by the military.

At the time that Ali was convicted for refusing to serve in Vietnam he was a member of the Nation of Islam. Elijah Muhammad, the Nation of Islam's leader, had been imprisoned himself for instructing his followers not to register for the draft during World War II. The Nation of Islam objected to African Americans being drafted to fight in defense of a country which continued to exploit and oppress African Americans. Isaac Woodard fought for America during World War II. His reward for doing so was being so brutally beaten by police officers that his eyes were damaged, and he was left blind. The Nation of Islam reasoned that it would be improper to kill and to die for a country which treated its African American veterans with such contempt. African Americans were expected to act violently in defense of America's interests, yet, as will be demonstrated, violence which was aimed at liberating African Americans from slavery and putting an end to racial oppression in the United

A Legally Created People

States was illegal and was often harshly punished.

In *Black Power*, Stokely Carmichael (Kwame Ture) and Charles Hamilton make the argument that drafting African people to participate in America's wars is an aspect of America's colonial domination of African people. They explain: "Participation of black men in the white man's wars is a characteristic of colonialism. The colonial ruler readily calls upon and expects the subject to fight and die in defense of the colonial empire, without the ruler feeling any particular compulsion to grant the subjects equal status." This was certainly true for African Americans and those who objected to being called to fight and die in defense of America's empire were imprisoned for doing so.

There were very few legal methods for enslaved Africans to secure their freedom. The inability to vote meant that the enslaved obviously could not vote for candidates who opposed slavery. In other words, there was no possibility of the enslaved voting to end their enslavement. There is also the fact that a significant number of presidents were slave owners, so those who were in positions of political power had a vested interest in continuing the institution of slavery because they were benefitting from that institution.

Some enslaved Africans opted to use the judicial system to fight for their freedom. Elizabeth Key Grinstead sued and won her freedom in 1656 in Virginia, which was still a British colony at the time. Elizabeth was born to an enslaved African mother and a free white father named Thomas Key. In her trial, Elizabeth asserted that she was the daughter of a free English subject and that on this basis she was born free. Elizabeth's suit was a success and she was granted her freedom.

Elizabeth later married a white man named William Grinstead. Her descendants came to be classified as "white" under the law in Virginia. One descendant, John Grinstead, was not only listed as white, but was also the owner of thirty-one slaves as well. This demonstrated the racial hierarchy of the American legal system. Had Key not been born to a white father she would have had little hope of prevailing in her claim, but not only did she prevail, her descendants came to profit from the very system of slavery which Elizabeth had managed to escape from. In essence, Elizabeth managed to escape slavery and her descendants managed to escape blackness.

In *Hudgins v. Wright*, 1 Hen. & M. 134 (1806), the Wrights were able to successfully obtain their freedom. The reasoning which Judge Tucker of the Supreme Court of Appeals of Virginia provided for ruling that the Wrights were to be freed demonstrated the racial attitudes surrounding slavery at the time. The Wrights appeared white and were descendants of a free Native American woman. Judge Tucker explained that if a black or mulatto woman were to appear before a judge on the writ of habeas corpus, on the ground of false imprisonment and detention in slavery, the judge "must redeliver the black or mulatto person, with the flat nose and woolly hair to the person claiming to hold him or her as a slave, unless the black person or mulatto could procure some person to be bound for him, to produce proof of his descent, in the maternal line, from a *free female ancestor.*" Judge Tucker also explained that the first clause of the Bill of Rights "was meant to embrace the case of free citizens, or aliens only; and not by a side wind to overturn the rights of property, and give freedom to those very people whom we have been compelled from imperious circumstances to retain, generally, in the same state of bondage that they were in at the revolution, in which they had no *concern, agency* or *interest.*"

Lawsuits on the part of the enslaved were not always successful. In *Queen v. Hepburn*, 11 U.S. 290 (1813), the Supreme Court ruled on the case of Mima Queen, who sued for freedom. The Supreme Court ultimately ruled against Mima because she relied on hearsay to prove that Mary, the ancestor of the Mima, was captured from Africa and taken to America. The plaintiffs read the deposition of Richard Disney, who stated that he heard that Captain Larkin brought Mary to America. The plaintiffs also read the deposition of Thomas Warfield, who stated that John Jiams, an inspector of tobacco, told him that Mary was free and was brought into America by Captain Larkin, and was sold for seven years. Neither Disney nor Warfield were speaking from their own knowledge, but from what they had been told.

Suits for freedom were successful in some cases, but not always. Moreover, such suits only freed the individuals who were bringing the suit for freedom, but those suits left the institution of slavery intact. In *Dred Scott v. Sandford*, 60 U.S. (19 How.) 393 (1857), the Supreme Court held that African people did not have any rights which a white man was bound to respect. Chief Justice Roger Taney, who delivered the opinion of the Supreme Court, explained that Africans "had for more than a century before been regarded as beings of an inferior order, and altogether unfit to associate with the white race either in social or political relations, and so far inferior that they had no rights which the white man was bound to respect, and that the negro might justly and lawfully be reduced to slavery for his benefit. He was bought and sold, and treated as an ordinary article of merchandise and traffic whenever a profit could be made by it." Based on this reasoning, the Supreme Court held that Dred Scott did not have standing to bring a suit in federal court.

Some enslaved Africans opted for rebellion and resistance, which was illegal. Nat Turner was executed for leading a violent slave uprising, which led to the murders of several white people, including women and children. Denmark Vesey and Gabriel Prosser did not even get a chance to execute their uprisings. Both men were executed merely for plotting slave uprisings, which were later exposed before they could be carried out. White slave masters were free to torture, rape, mutilate, and even kill the enslaved, but the enslaved could not rebel and inflict some of those same harms on white people without suffering reprisals for doing so.

Nat Turner's rebellion is especially noteworthy because this rebellion alarmed slave master so much that some defenders of slavery were openly calling for the enforcement of laws to prevent future rebellions like the one that Nat Turner led. An editorial in the Richmond *Enquirer* from August 30,

1831 stated: "The case of Nat Turner warns us. No black man ought to be permitted to turn preacher through the country. The law must be enforced, or the tragedy of Southampton appeals to us in vain." Of course, as will be addressed later, there already were laws in place to protect slave masters because of the massive slave uprising in Haiti, but Turner's rebellion demonstrated that further restrictions were still needed to protect slave masters from their property.

Whereas acts of violence on the part of the enslaved were regarded as being criminal acts for which the enslaved could be punished, slave masters were often free to do as they pleased to the enslaved. This is demonstrated in the case of *State v. Mann*, 2 Dev. 263 (1829), which was tried by the Supreme Court of North Carolina. In this case, the defendant was indicted for an assault and battery upon Lydia, the slave of a woman named Elizabeth Jones. The battery occurred during the period in which Lydia was hired by the defendant to work as a slave.

The opinion of the Court was delivered by Judge Thomas Ruffin, who applied the property concept of bailment. Bailment refers to when personal property is transferred from the owner of the property in question (the bailor) to another (the bailee). The bailee takes temporary possession of the property. The question before the Supreme Court in this case was "whether a cruel and unreasonable battery on a slave, by the hirer, is indictable." Since Lydia, a slave, was regarded as a property, the question in this case was not a matter of a criminal case of assault and battery, but rather a matter of whether or not the bailee in this situation could be indicted for battery against a piece of property which the bailee held temporary possession of, but did not own.

The Supreme Court of North Carolina did recognize that there were some cases in which a battery committed on a slave could be an indictable offense. In *State v. Hale*, 2 Hawks 582 (1823), the Supreme Court of North Carolina held that indictment is maintainable in situations where a slave has been the victim of a battery, although the Court also held that not every case of battery against a slave is indictable. Chief Justice Taylor, who delivered the opinion of the Court, noted that battery "must be considered with a view to the actual condition of society, and the difference between a white man and a slave, securing the first from injury and insult, and the other from needless violence and outrage." The Supreme Court of North Carolina had made it very apparent that battery against a white man was not the same as a battery against a slave. In his concurrence, Judge Hall stated that "it would be highly improper that every assault and battery upon a slave should be considered an indictable offence; because the person making it, might have matter of excuse or justification on his side, which could not be used as a defence for committing an assault and battery upon a free person."

In *The State v. Mann*, Justice Ruffin noted that the laws of North Carolina "uniformly treat the master or other person having the possession and command of the slave, as entitled to the same extent of authority." Ruffin continued to explain that "the general owner, the hirer and possessor of a slave, in relation to both rights and duties, is, for the time being, the owner." In other words, a person who comes into possession of a slave has all of the same rights and duties regarding that slave that the slave's master would have. After all, a slave was legally regarded as a piece of property and as such the bailee has all of the same rights to the use of that property as the bailor has.

One right which courts were willing to recognize and uphold was the right of the master to do whatever was necessary to secure the submission of the slave. As Justice Ruffin explained: "The power of the master must be absolute, to render the submission of the slave perfect." This meant even the use of physical force if necessary. Given that the right to secure the submission of a slave was one which courts were willing to recognize for the slave master, such rights were accorded to a bailee as well given that the bailee may also need to resort to violence to secure the submission of the slave. Justice Ruffin concluded that so long as slavery exists "it will be the imperative duty of the Judges to recognise the full dominion of the owner over the slave, except where the exercise of it is forbidden by statute." For this reason, the Court ruled in favor of the defendant.

In explaining the Court's decision, Justice Ruffin wrote that "dominion is essential to the value of slaves as property, to the security of the master, and the public [tranquility], greatly dependent upon their subordination; and in fine, as most effectually securing the general protection and comfort of the slaves themselves." This passage is important for two reasons. The first of which is that it very clearly articulates the view that slaves are property. Secondly, the passage indicates that the submission of a slave was seen as being necessary for public tranquility, as well as for the protection and comfort of the slaves themselves.

Resorting to physical force was seen as being necessary because of the fear that if slaves became too rebellious it could pose a serious threat to public tranquility. Indeed, slave masters often lived in dread of the possibility of a massive slave uprising, especially after the rebellion in Haiti completely overturned the slave system there, liberating Haitians from French rule and establishing an independent black republic.

This fear of Haiti was such that some states began to pass laws to prevent a similar uprising. South Carolina passed a law in 1800 which stipulated: "It shall not be lawful for any number of slaves, free Negroes, mulattoes, or mestizoes, even in company with white persons, to meet together and assemble for the purpose of mental instruction or religious worship either before the rising of the sun or after the going down of the same." The prior mentioned plots by Gabriel Prosser and Denmark Vesey, and Turner's rebellion also contributed to the implementation of laws which were designed to prevent violent slave uprising.

Both Vesey and Turner relied on religious sentiment to organize their rebellions. One account gave the following description of Vesey: "Like many of his race, he possessed the gift of gab, as the silver in the tongue and the gold in the full or thick-lipped mouth are oftentimes contemptuously characterized.

And, like many of his race, he was a devoted student of the Bible, to whose interpretation he brought, like many other Bible students not confined to the Negro race, a good deal of imagination and not a little of superstition, which, with some natures, is perhaps but another name for the desires of the heart." Vesey benefited from the fact that by 1822, the laws in South Carolina regarding African meetings were not as rigorously enforced as they had been in the past.

Vesey's plot was well-organized, but he was betrayed. Nat Turner did manage to execute his plans, however. Nat Turner's parents were very religious, and one account stated that as a child he was taught by his mother that "he was born, like Moses, to be the deliverer of his race." The account further explained: "It is said that he never laughed. He was a dreamy sort of a man, and avoided the crowd." As a result of Nat Turner's rebellion, laws were passed which restricted the ability of Africans, freed or enslaved, to preach. For example, in Mississippi, a law was passed which stated that it was "unlawful for any slave, free Negro, or mulatto to preach the gospel" upon pain of receiving thirty-nine lashes upon the naked back of anyone who violated this law.

There was also Harriet Tubman, who ran away from the slave plantation. Tubman, who was never captured, made several trips back to rescue others, which was a very clear violation of the law. Given that slaves were regarded as property, Tubman's actions were tantamount to the theft of property. After Tubman's death Booker T. Washington would, somewhat ironically, praise

Harriet Tubman as being an example of a "law-abiding" black woman, but the reality is that she was not. Harriet Tubman was a criminal, as were most of the slaves who rebelled against their enslavement. Slavery was the law and therefore to be law-abiding within that context meant respecting the institution of slavery.

To be clear, aiding slaves in escaping to freedom was a violation of the law. This was the issue which came up in *Ableman v. Booth*, 62 U.S. (21 How.) 506 (1859), in which the Supreme Court held that fugitive slave laws were constitutional and that state courts had to abide by such laws. Sherman Booth was charged with aiding and abetting in the escape of a fugitive slave. Booth sought a writ of habeas corpus from a Wisconsin state judge, which was granted. Booth was subsequently released after the judge decided that Booth's detention was illegal.

Stephen Ableman, a United States marshal, appealed to the state supreme court, which ruled that the federal law was unconstitutional and affirmed Booth's release. The case eventually came before the United States Supreme Court, which overturned the Supreme Court of Wisconsin's decision to free Sherman. The issue raised in this particular case was that the Supreme Court of Wisconsin did not have the authority to go beyond the limits of the powers which were conferred to the Supreme Court of Wisconsin by the federal government.

The ruling in *Ableman* upheld the constitutionality of the fugitive slave act which Booth was charged with violating. The Supreme Court held that "it is proper to say that, in the judgment of this court, the act of Congress commonly called the fugitive slave law is, in all of its provisions, fully authorized by the Constitution of the United States, that the commissioner had lawful authority to issue the warrant and commit the party, and that his proceedings were regular and conformable to law." The ruling in *Ableman* also affirmed the legality of slavery and those individuals, such as Sherman Booth, who were engaged in the work of helping enslaved individuals to escape from the bondage of slavery were in violation of the law.

Slavery was abolished in the United States following the Civil War. Congress then adopted several amendments which established citizenship and equal rights for the former slaves. The Thirteenth, Fourteenth, and Fifteenth Amendments were ratified for the purpose of abolishing slavery, granting African Americans citizenship, and granting African Americans equal voting rights. Malcolm X pointed to the ineffectiveness of these amendments which were designed to resolve the race problem, stating: "Some more white liberals came along with the Thirteenth, Fourteenth, and [Fifteenth] amendments, which were supposed to solve the race problem. The problem is still here."

The significance of what Malcolm was pointing out here is the fact that laws which were passed to address racial inequality failed to completely achieve their objectives. What often happened was that new laws which were designed to address racism in America were undermined through a variety of ways, including rulings by the Supreme Court which upheld racial segregation. Therefore, the issue was not necessarily the lack of adequate legislation regarding racism, but the fact that the United States did not truly intend for the African population to enjoy equal rights. For this reason, whatever rights were passed for the purpose of addressing the racial problem in America were not strongly enforced.

The Supreme Court's ruling in *Plessy v. Ferguson*, 163 U.S. 537 (1896) demonstrated the Court's unwillingness to enforce the provisions of the Fourteenth Amendment. The suit in *Plessy* was brought by a citizen who was described as being one-eight African, though the Supreme Court noted that the mixture of colored blood was not discernible in him. The petitioner was a resident of Louisiana who paid for a first class passage on the East Louisiana Railway. He sat down in a part of the train which was reserved for white people only. He was subsequently ejected by force and jailed.

The case turned on the constitutionality of an act passed in Louisiana in 1890, which provided for separate railway carriages for the white and colored races. The first section of the statute provides "that all railway companies carrying passengers in their coaches in this State, shall provide equal but separate accommodations for the white, and colored races, by providing two or more passenger coaches for each passenger train, or by dividing the passenger coaches by a partition so as to secure separate accommodations: *Provided*, That this section shall not be construed to apply to street railroads. No person or persons, shall be admitted to occupy seats in coaches, other than, the ones, assigned, to them on account of the race they belong to."

A Legally Created People

The Supreme Court held that Louisiana's segregation law did not violate the Thirteenth Amendment because implying a legal distinction between white and colored races "has no tendency to destroy the legal equality of the two races, or reestablish a state of involuntary servitude." Regarding the Fourteenth Amendment, the Supreme Court held that the amendment "could not have been intended to abolish distinctions based upon color, or to enforce social, as distinguished from political equality, or a commingling of the two races upon terms unsatisfactory to either."

The ruling in *Plessy* helped to lay a foundation for racist Jim Crow laws which enforced racial segregation and racial inequality. Plessy implemented the doctrine of "separate but equal." This meant that segregation could exist so long as African Americans were given equal access to everything which white citizens enjoyed. "Separate but equal" was a mere legal fiction which was implemented to uphold the constitutionality of racial segregation. The reality is that there was no equality in segregation. How could there be when the restrictions which were being placed on African Americans were not placed on white citizens, who enjoyed more freedoms and privileges.

Recall that in the two previously mentioned cases in which enslaved persons were able to sue and win their freedom, one of the factors that worked in their favor was having non-African ancestry. In *Plessy*, however, the Supreme Court not only upheld racial segregation, but it also upheld the one-drop rule, which stated that anyone with any trace of African ancestry was black and therefore subjected to all of the same racial restrictions which were placed upon black people. Therefore, the ruling not only established the legality of racial segregation, but also further entrenched the one-drop rule and made it so that even persons of mixed racial ancestry were also denied equal rights.

In time, the Supreme Court would later overturn these racist policies in *Brown v. Board of Education of Topeka*, 347 U.S. 483 (1954). In *Brown* the Supreme Court held that school segregation was unconstitutional. This was a significant blow to racial segregation in America, as this ruling overturned the "separate but equal" doctrine of *Plessy*. The issue before the Supreme Court in *Brown* was the fact that segregated public schools could not be equal. The Court noted: "The plaintiffs contend that segregated public schools are not 'equal' and cannot be made 'equal,' and that hence they are deprived of the equal protection of the laws."

The leaders of the civil rights movement decided that they would struggle to change the law by breaking the law. The struggles of A.N.C. in South Africa were previously mentioned as an example of a situation in which individuals resorted to breaking the law in order to change the law. In both the United States and South Africa, racial discrimination and racial inequality were codified into law. Therefore, such laws needed to be defied because of the unjust nature of those laws. In both situations, individuals were often arrested and jailed for these acts of defiance.

One of the seminal moments of the civil rights

movement was the arrest of Rosa Parks. Parks was arrested in 1955 for refusing to give up her seat on a bus to white passengers. The fact that Parks was arrested demonstrates the illegality of even mild forms of resistance against racist policies. In this case, by refusing to move from her seat, Rosa Parks was taking a defiant stance against the segregation laws which were enforced on public transportation in Alabama. Parks' arrest sparked the Montgomery bus boycott which eventually led to the development of a national civil rights movement.

Alabama's segregation laws became the subject of *Browder v. Gayle*, 142 F. Supp. 707 (1956). This was a case brought by four African American plaintiffs who were arrested and fined for failing to comply with Alabama's segregationist laws. The district court held that "the statutes and ordinances requiring segregation of the white and colored races on the motor buses of a common carrier of passengers in the City of Montgomery and its police jurisdiction violate the due process and equal protection of the law clauses of the Fourteenth Amendment to the Constitution of the United States."

One of the accomplishments of the civil rights movement was that it was able to successfully change many of the laws which were put in place to uphold racial segregation. Doing so was not an easy process, however. Putting an end to Alabama's segregation laws involved open defiance to those laws, which resulted in individuals being arrested and fined. It also involved an organized boycott to put economic pressure on segregated bus companies.

Ultimately, the judicial system did rule against Alabama's segregation laws, but the challenge to these segregation laws was more than merely a legal challenge. This challenge involved acts of civil disobedience in which individuals had decided that they would refuse to comply with the segregation laws, opting to be arrested and fined instead.

Alabama became the center of another legal dispute regarding segregation. John Patterson, the Attorney General of Alabama, brought a suit to enjoin the National Association for the Advancement of Colored People (N.A.A.C.P.) from conducting further activity in the state and to oust the N.A.A.C.P. from Alabama. One of the issues raised by Patterson was that the N.A.A.C.P. "had supported a Negro boycott of the bus lines in Montgomery to compel the seating of passengers without regard to race."

The state of Alabama moved for the production of a large number of the N.A.A.C.P.'s records, including the names and addresses of all of the N.A.A.C.P.'s members in Alabama. The case came before the Supreme Court. In *National Association for the Advancement of Colored People v. Alabama*, 357 U.S. 449 (1958), the Supreme Court held "that the immunity from state scrutiny of membership lists which the Association claims on behalf of its members is here so related to the right of the members to pursue their lawful private interests privately and to associate freely with others in so doing as to come within the protection of the Fourteenth Amendment." Justice John Marshall Harlan, who delivered the Supreme Court's opinion, also noted "that Alabama has fallen short of showing a controlling justification for the deterrent effect on the free enjoyment of the right to associate which disclosure of membership lists is likely to have."

One question which emerges from civil disobedience and other acts of direct violation of an existing law is where does one draw the line between laws which should be challenged and laws which should be respected? More specifically stated, if the Supreme Court ruling in *Plessy* upholds segregation and was therefore challenged by the civil rights movement, how then can activists in the civil rights movement ask others to respect the Supreme Court ruling in *Brown*? Why should some laws or rulings be more respected than others?

Martin Luther King wrote his well-known "Letter from Birmingham Jail" while in jail in 1963 during his Birmingham campaign. In the letter, King not only defended his civil disobedience tactics, but he also explained that he felt that it was just for one to resist unjust laws. King acknowledged that he encouraged some laws to be followed, even though he consciously broke other laws. King explained:

Since we so diligently urge people to obey the Supreme Court's decision of 1954 outlawing segregation in the public schools, at first glance it may seem rather paradoxical for us consciously to break laws. One may well ask: "How can you advocate breaking some laws and obeying others?" The answer lies in the fact that there are two types of laws: just and unjust. I would be the first to advocate obeying just laws. One has not only a legal but a moral responsibility to obey just laws.

Based on the abovementioned passage from King one may ask who determines which laws are unjust and which are just? We certainly know that when the United States was formed, slavery was legal. In the view of some, slavery was just. Rev. Charles C. Jones, a defender of slavery, wrote of the period from 1790 until 1820 that "the religious and physical condition of the Negroes were both improved during this period. Their increase was natural and regular, ranging every ten years between thirty-four and thirty-six per cent. As the old stock from Africa died out of the country, the grosser customs, ignorance, and paganism of Africa died with them. Their descendants, the country-born, were better looking, more intelligent, more civilized, more susceptible of religious impressions." In the view of some whites, slavery was a benefit to African people and therefore slavery was just in their view. Of course, many of the Africans who endured the hardships of slavery would not have shared this positive view of slavery.

The oppressed will have a different view of the law than the oppressor will because the oppressed are the ones who feel the brunt of these laws. Naturally, this leads to a clash between the oppressed and the oppressor over these laws. King and others in the civil rights movement certainly had a different view of Jim Crow laws than did the likes of Bull Connor or James Eastland. This led to a clash between those who wished to uphold segregation laws and those who fought to change those laws.

The United States was founded by European

settlers who were primarily concerned with their own interests. The well-being of African people was a secondary concern and America's laws reflected this. Laws which may have seemed just to a white man who benefitted from slavery and white supremacy would not be seen as just to an African who was victimized by such laws. In this regard, a law being just or unjust is, in some respects, a matter of perspective. When the United States was founded, the perspectives and concerns of African people were of little consideration to the founders. Africans were, as the Supreme Court explained in *Dred Scott v. Sandford*, "articles of merchandise" and therefore were not given the same rights as white citizens.

Within the context of the struggle of African Americans, a just law should be understood as a law which asserts the humanity of African people and helps to advance the interests of African people as a group. The reasoning behind this is that if it is considered just for white people to have the right to life, liberty, and the pursuit of happiness, then African people should also have these same rights as well. Therefore, a just law is a law which gives equal rights to all people, regardless of racial background. Any law which is designed to deny African people rights which are afforded to white citizens are laws which are not only unjust, but which exist for the purpose of maintaining the oppression of African people.

The very reason why Africans have had to rebel against American laws is precisely because the laws that were in place were laws which denied Africans the right to life, liberty, and the pursuit of happiness.

This is the same reason why Americans rebelled against British colonial rule and established an independent nation. The leaders of the American Revolution certainly were not as dehumanized and oppressed as Africans in the United States have been, but they were unwilling to tolerate what they perceived to be a denial of fundamental human rights. Africans in the United States have had to confront the fact that America is a nation which was born out of the revolutionary struggle of European settlers who wanted liberty but did not wish to extend this liberty to enslaved Africans. African people were expected to passively accept being enslaved because submission to oppression was the only way for an African to be lawful within an unjust legal system. It is for this reason that unjust laws can also be understood as laws which punish individuals who attempt to struggle for their liberty.

King himself was well-aware that freedom and liberty are things which must be struggled for. In his letter he explained: "We know through painful experience that freedom is never voluntarily given by the oppressor; it must be demanded by the oppressed." To those who would suggest that African Americans patiently wait for change to come, King responded: "We have waited for more than 340 years for our constitutional and God given rights."

King's reference to constitutional rights demonstrated that King believed that the rights provided by the Constitution were rights that were owed to African Americans. Malcolm X held a different view. Whereas King held the view that

A Legally Created People

Africans in the United States were American citizens who had been denied the rights that are due to American citizens, Malcolm held the view that Africans in the United States were not citizens nor were they even Americans. Malcolm stated: "We are African, and we happen to be in America. We're not Americans. We are a people who formerly were Africans who were kidnaped and brought to America." For this reason, Malcolm expressed the view that African Americans should not rely on the American government to solve the race problem because it was the government which was responsible for the problem in the first place. This is why Malcolm's position was that the problem that African Americans confronted was a human rights problem, not a civil rights problem.

After his separation from the Nation of Islam, Malcolm began speaking about taking the struggle of African Americans before the United Nations. Malcolm felt that the problem was beyond America's ability to solve, so he argued that the problem should be taken out of the jurisdiction of America's courts and brought before an international court.

In his biography of Malcolm X, Manning Marable asserted that the "United Nations World Conference Against Racism, held in Durban, South Africa in 2001, was in many ways a fulfillment of Malcolm's international vision," which is a view that Abdul Alkalimat described as ridiculous. Alkalimat explained that "Malcolm X would have condemned the Durban meeting just as he did the 1963 March on Washington." Alkalimat continued on to explain that Malcolm "would have predicted what actually happened in Durban: The U.S. imperialists blocked any open debate in order to defend their client state, Israel."

America's strong influence within the United Nations is certainly one obstacle which Malcolm would have confronted. The United States is one of five permanent members of the Security Council of the United Nations along with Russia, China, France, and Britain. Each one of these five members has veto power, which would prevent the adoption of any Council resolution. For this reason, the U.N. would not have been able to adopt a resolution which was too critical of America.

To digress away from the topic of the African American struggle for equal rights under the law, some remarks must be made about the United Nations World Conference Against Racism to demonstrate the potential of utilizing international entities in the struggle against racism. Malcolm was assassinated before he could truly implement his ideas, but the Brazilian activist and psychologist Edna Roland offers an example of what utilizing the United Nations could accomplish.

Alkalimat is correct in pointing out that the United States blocked open debate at the conference in order to defend Israel, but critical discussions on the topic of racism were not blocked at this conference. It was at this conference that Roland addressed the issue of racism against African people, as well as reparations for the harms caused by racism.

The news that Roland, a psychologist, had been made a rapporteur for the conference in Durban was a surprise to other psychologists in Brazil, as well as a source of pride. Although Roland is a psychologist by profession, Roland also described herself as an activist of the black movement and an activist in the struggle for human rights in Brazil. Roland was one of the many activists who opposed the military dictatorship in Brazil.

Through her work with the United Nations, Roland was able to advocate not only for reparations, but also for policies which address the problem of racism against African people in Brazil. Much of Roland's organizing activities have also centered around the U.N.'s efforts to address racism. The U.N. declared the International Decade for People of African Descent, which began in 2015. One of the activities which the Coordination of Racial Equality of the Prefecture of Guarulhos—of which Roland was involved in—organized for the International Decade of People of African Descent was a march against racism which was organized to take place every year on November 20th, which is Black Awareness Day in Brazil. Black Awareness Day is a day which honors the rebel leader Zumbi. Roland also participated in the inauguration of AFROMADRID, which was organized in 2015 for the International Decade for People of African Descent.

Roland also appeared on a program with Congresswoman Ana Alencar to discuss the Special Secretariat for the Promotion of Racial Equality which was created by the government of Brazil for the purpose of participating in discussions regarding the Racial Equality Statute. The program discussed the International Day for the End of Racial

Discrimination on March 21. This day was created by the U.N. to commemorate the Sharpeville Massacre in South Africa. The Secretariat for the Promotion of Racial Equality in Brazil decided to extend the commemoration of this occasion until March 25.

Roland acknowledged that the abovementioned statute was conceived based on the problems confronting African people in Brazil, but she explained: "This does not mean that any other social group that is the victim of discrimination does not deserve attention from public policies. But it is necessary for us to pay attention to the specifics of the problem of each racial ethnic group." For Roland, this meant that the indigenous peoples must also be guaranteed their rights as well.

Roland was able to utilize the international platform offered by the United Nations to organize programs and events to address the problem of racism in Brazil. The Brazilian government itself adopted a more proactive position on addressing the racial issue in Brazil because of the U.N.'s efforts.

Malcolm stated that American democracy was hypocrisy. The struggles that those who were involved in the civil rights movement endured merely reinforced Malcolm's point. The Fourteenth Amendment to the Constitution was meant to provide citizenship to African Americans, who were previously deemed to be non-citizens, yet, when King and others began to march and demonstrate for the rights that are due to American citizens they were met with aggression from those who sought to uphold racial inequality in America. This hypocrisy was further highlighted by the fact that, as Malcolm pointed out, President John F. Kennedy took no action to protect the protesters in Birmingham who were being brutalized by police officers. It was only when African Americans became frustrated with the situation and began violently rioting that President Kennedy decided to send troops to Birmingham to quell the situation.

It was very apparent that the American legal system had little interest in protecting the civil rights or the safety of African Americans. The hardships that King endured serve to demonstrate this point. Unlike the Nation of Islam, King did not advocate for racial separation as a solution to racism in America. And unlike Malcolm X, King completely rejected any notion of violent self-defense. King's approach to the problem was to appeal to America's morality and to America's founding principles through a campaign of nonviolent civil disobedience. King's campaign helped to expose the viciousness of segregation in America, as men, women, and even children who were peacefully demanding equal rights were met with violent force because although those in the civil rights movement were demonstrating peacefully, their actions were still illegal and therefore many of them were treated as criminals.

In his letter, King offered an answer to the question of how to determine whether or not a law is unjust. King wrote: "A just law is a man made code that squares with the moral law or the law of God. An unjust law is a code that is out of harmony with the moral law." King also explained that a just law is a law that is rooted in eternal law and natural law. Based on this definition, King concludes that segregation laws are unjust. He writes: "Any law that degrades human personality is unjust. All segregation statutes are unjust because segregation distorts the soul and damages the personality. It gives the segregator a false sense of superiority and the segregated a false sense of inferiority."

King urged individuals to obey the Supreme Court decision of 1954 because the ruling of the Supreme Court was just. That ruling, as noted before, held that segregated educational facilities are unconstitutional. In doing so, the Supreme Court struck a blow against its previous ruling in *Plessy*, which upheld racial segregation. The 1954 ruling was more beneficial for African Americans than the ruling in *Plessy* was. For this reason, the ruling in 1954 can be seen as a just ruling because it improved the ability of African Americans to gain access to a quality education, which was deliberately denied through segregationist policies.

King explained that there "are some instances when a law is just on its face and unjust in its application." The example that King presents was his own arrest for "parading without a permit." King acknowledges that there is nothing wrong with an ordinance which requires a permit for a parade," but he also adds that "when the ordinance is used to preserve segregation and to deny citizens the First Amendment privilege of peaceful assembly and peaceful protest, then it becomes unjust."

There are times when an unjust law may seem just on its face, but, as King rightly notes, the just or unjust nature of that law is ultimately determined by the manner in which the law is enforced. In the case of laws which require a permit for large public gatherings, such laws may not be inherently unjust, but when such laws are used to prevent people from gathering to demonstrate against unjust laws then those laws become unjust laws. It is not uncommon that unjust laws are implemented with the pretense that such laws exist to protect the peace. We have already seen examples of laws which were passed to prevent slave uprisings. Such laws were not only implemented to keep the peace and prevent outbursts of violence, but to also keep enslaved Africans subjugated. Of course, were it not for the fact that Africans were subjugated under slavery there would be no reason for Africans to rebel. Likewise, were it not for racist segregation laws, King and others would not have had to assemble to protest against segregation, so very often the unjust laws create the very problem which the law claims to be trying to prevent.

In his letter, King also pointed out that everything that Adolf Hitler did in Germany was legal. This point here is critical to understanding King's views on just laws and unjust laws. The laws which were implemented in Nazi Germany under Hitler's reign were clearly unjust, as such policies led to the massacre of millions of Jews and Hitler's aggressive actions eventually led to a war which killed over 70 million people. Despite this, the actions which were undertaken by the Nazis were legal because the Nazis were in power and had the ability to implement laws as they saw fit.

The legality of an action does not determine the morality or justness of said action. It has been demonstrated that African people in the United Stated have often had to engage in illegal actions to assert their rights and advance their interests, yet one can hardly say that Harriet Tubman was behaving unjustly or immorally for assisting slaves with escaping to freedom.

The example of Nazi Germany also provides an international context for understanding this situation because although the focus thus far has been the plight of Africans in the United States, people of African descent globally have faced oppression which was inflicted by European societies. This oppression of African people was often justified due to a belief in the racial superiority of white people, which is the very thing that the Nazis in Germany preached.

The fact is that the genocidal violence which Nazi Germany engaged in was not unique. For centuries European nations were engaged in acts of genocide as well. Millions of Native Americans were killed off as the result of European colonization and expansion throughout the Americas. The slave trade resulted in the deaths of millions of Africans. The colonization of Africa led to the deaths of millions more. Before the Jewish Holocaust, the Germans had carried out an act of genocide against African people in nation of Namibia, known then as German South West Africa. The massacre of millions of Jews in Germany resulted not only in reparations being paid to the victims of the Holocaust, but also in the prosecution of many of the Nazis who were involved in the

Holocaust. The German massacre of Africans in German South West Africa did not invoke the same type of international outrage, however.

To return to the topic of laws in the United States, the civil rights movement did result in significant legal changes, namely the Civil Rights Act of 1964, which outlawed racial discrimination and the Voting Rights Act of 1965. Yet, as Malcolm X so accurately observed, legislation alone has not been enough to truly resolve the problem of racism in America. The situation in South Africa demonstrates this as well. The end of apartheid in South Africa was not the end of racial and economic inequality. Many of the institutions which upheld the brutal system of apartheid remained in place after Mandela was elected president. One of the clearest examples of this was the "Marikana massacre" in 2012, in which the security forces employed lethal force to put down a strike. This type of violent force aimed at silencing discontent among the citizens of South Africa was precisely the type of thing which the apartheid regime in South Africa was notorious for. In 2012, with the A.N.C. now in power, abuses of this nature continued. The civil rights movement and the struggle against apartheid demonstrate that oppressive and unjust systems can be very difficult to reform merely through altering laws to reduce some of the more blatantly racist features of the society. This is stated so that one understands that merely overturning an unjust law does not necessarily eliminate the system or the structures which inflict the injustices.

The facts presented demonstrate that when there

Wong (Omowale)

are no legal methods for oppressed people to achieve their liberty, the oppressed group often resorts to rebellion to obtain their liberty. Unjust laws must be challenged. Doing so not only means being able to distinguish an unjust law from a just law, but it also means understanding that challenging an unjust law is, by its very nature, an unlawful action. Yet, unlawful action is often the only recourse when society bars individuals from engaging in lawful activities to produce change.

Selected References:

Abdul Alkalimat, "Rethinking Malcolm Means First Learning How to Think: What Was Marable Thinking? And How?," *The Journal of Pan African Studies*, vol.5, no.1, March 2012.

Anton Lembede (author), Robert R. Edgar and Luyanda ka Msumza (editors) *Freedom in Our Lifetime*, 1996.

Booker T. Washington and W.E.B. Du Bois, *The Negro in the South*, 1907.

Nelson Mandela, *Long Walk to Freedom*, 1995.

Taunya Lovell Banks, "Dangerous Woman: Elizabeth Key's Freedom Suit-Subjecthood and Racialized Identity In Seventeenth Century Colonial Virginia," U of Maryland Legal Studies Research Paper No. 2005-28; Akron Law Review, v. 41, 2008, p. 799-837. (2008).

3 A LEGALLY CREATED PEOPLE

In *Psychopathic Racial Personality and Other Essays*, Bobby E. Wright argued that African Americans "are the world's only legally created group, (created through the 13th, 14th, and 15th amendments which can be repealed at any moment by the Congress or declared unconstitutional by the Supreme Court)." Wright's statement spoke to the very precarious legal situation which African Americans have been in. Congress has never repealed these amendments, but historically Congress has not consistently enforced the protections offered by these amendments. The Supreme Court has never declared the amendments unconstitutional, but the Supreme Court has certainly limited the protections offered by these amendments and has also limited the protections offered by civil rights legislation. In other words, Congress and the Supreme Court have not eliminated the legislation which was implemented to provide African Americans with the rights of citizenship, but such rights have been abridged so as to also protect the right of white people to discriminate as they see fit.

The Fourteenth Amendment was the amendment which provided citizenship for African Americans. The amendment reads:

> All persons born or naturalized in the United States, and subject to the jurisdiction thereof, are citizens of the United States and of the State wherein they reside. No State shall make or enforce any law which shall abridge the privileges or immunities of citizens of the United States; nor shall any State deprive any person of life, liberty, or property, without due process of law; nor deny to any person within its jurisdiction the equal protection of the laws.

The Fourteenth Amendment, in theory, provided equal status for African Americans. In practice, however, African Americans continued to endure racism and the deprivation of the rights which white citizens enjoyed. This has even included white immigrant groups who arrived in the United States after African Americans did. Although some European immigrant groups such as Italians and Irish did endure discrimination and prejudice in America, African Americans have been the group that has been consistently denied of their constitutional rights, to such an extent that it has required several amendments to the Constitution and the passage of civil right laws to protect the constitutional rights of African Americans; rights which are due to American citizens at birth.

A Legally Created People

Consider the fact that the Constitution itself had to be altered to provide more protections to African Americans. The Constitution had to be amended just so that persons of African descent who were born free in the United States could be regarded as being equal with white citizens. Consider the numerous civil rights bills that were passed for the purpose of providing equal treatment and equal protection to African Americans. This is what Bobby E. Wright referred to when he stated that African Americans were a legally created people. It took the alteration of American law for African Americans to be regarded as equals under that very law. This created a separate legal status for African Americans, which was much different from the legal status of white citizens.

The struggle to obtain equal citizenship rights must also be understood in economic terms as well because the exploitation of African Americans was not merely a form of racial oppression, but a form of economic oppression as well; a type of oppression which benefited the financial interests of white citizens. African people were dragged to the United States for the purpose of being enslaved. African people did not willingly go to America to be worked as slaves. Moreover, slavery was an industry which many individuals profited from. Slaves were a commodity, which were bought and sold on auction blocks. The slave also worked for the slave master without pay.

The primary reason why Africans were brought to the United States was to be utilized for slave labor. For this reason, when the United States was founded, the laws which were implemented were laws which were consistent with America's slave society. The laws were also consistent with the white supremacist views held by some of the Founding Fathers. Thomas Jefferson, for example, expressed the view that "the blacks, whether originally a distinct race, or made distinct by time and circumstances, are inferior to the whites in the endowments both of body and mind."

The United States was not formed with the interests and the well-being of African people being a central focus. This was so painfully true that despite the horrible conditions which enslaved Africans had to endure inside of the slave ships which brought them to America, the Constitution ensured that the slave trade would be protected until 1801. Article 1, Section 9, Clause 1 reads: "The Migration or Importation of such Persons as any of the States now existing shall think proper to admit, shall not be prohibited by the Congress prior to the Year one thousand eight hundred and eight, but a Tax or duty may be imposed on such Importation, not exceeding ten dollars for each Person."

Newly liberated Africans were now making the transition away from being commodities in a slave society to being laborers in a capitalistic society. Slavery itself had played a significant role in the development of Western capitalism. This is a point that Eric Williams documented in his book *Capitalism and Slavery*. Unlike slaves, the worker in a capitalistic system is not owned by a master. In the system of capitalism, a worker freely contracts to provide his or her laborer to an employer who pays the worker a wage in return for the worker's labor. Whereas a slave is made to work against his or her will—often through the threat of force—the worker is compelled to work because the worker needs to earn a wage in order to pay for necessities such as food and shelter.

In the relationship between the employer and the employee, the employer generally maintains the dominant position. One does not have to adhere to Karl Marx's theories to understand that within the system of capitalism contradictions between the worker and the employer can and do arise. Marx envisioned that the working class would one day rebel against the capitalist ruling class and that this revolution would bring forward a communist society in which the means of production are commonly owned by the workers themselves rather than being owned and controlled by a few capitalists who profit from the labor of the working class.

America was never subjected to the type of communist inspired revolution which Russia experienced, but America certainly has not been immune to struggles between the working class and the owners of the means of production. The dangers of unrestrained capitalism are precisely why Marx envisioned an eventual uprising on the part of the working class, which would overturn the exploitative capitalist system. Such a revolution may very well have been inevitable in industrialized capitalist countries if not for reforms and regulations which restrict the power of the employer and provide protections for the employee. Far from overturning a system in which the working class labors for wages, the reforms ensure that the working class is not overworked and underpaid. These regulations have also ensured that children cannot be employed to work as laborers and that workers can be compensated if they are injured while working.

African people found themselves oppressed not only within a society that implemented a very strict racial hierarchy, but also a system with a class hierarchy as well. It is for this reason that civil rights legislation can be understood to be not only about protecting African Americans from racial discrimination, but also about protecting working people from being exploited by their employers. After all, an African who was denied a job on account of his or her race was not only being discriminated against racially but was also a victim of a capitalist system which places the worker at the mercy of the employer. Again, one does not need to adhere to the theories of Marx to understand that in an economic system where one's survival is based on the ability to earn a wage from an employer, there is an inherent inequality that can be easily exploited to the benefit of the employer and to the detriment of the employee.

The Supreme Court has often struggled with maintaining the balance between allowing capitalists to freely engage in the pursuit of enriching themselves and regulating businesses for the purpose of protecting the interests of workers. Where the two interests clashed, there were times when the Supreme Court took the side of the capitalist employer over that of the worker. This was very apparent during the so-called Lochner Era. This era is so called because of *Lochner v. New York*, 198 U.S. 45 (1905), which was a case in which the Supreme Court struck down a New York state law that regulated the working hours of bakers. *Lochner* was one of several cases in which the Supreme Court struck down measures that were implemented to improve the conditions of American workers.

In *Lochner*, Justice Rufus Peckham, who delivered the opinion, declared that the "general right to make a contract in relation to his business is part of the liberty of the individual protected by the Fourteenth Amendment of the Federal Constitution." Justice Peckham continued to explain that the "right to purchase or to sell labor is part of the liberty protected by this amendment, unless there are circumstances which exclude the right." The Supreme Court in *Lochner* held that working hours for bakers was not one of those circumstances where the right to purchase and sell labor should be abridged. Justice Peckham explained: "There is no reasonable ground for interfering with the liberty of person or the right of free contract, by determining the hours of labor, in the occupation of a baker."

Justice Peckham cited *Holden v. Hardy*, 169 U.S. 366 (1989) which was a case in which the Supreme Court held that a law limiting the work hours of miners and smelters was a valid exercise of police power by the State, but Justice Peckham explained that the ruling in *Holden* did not apply in *Lochner*. Peckham explained that the law limiting the work hours of bakers was not related to protecting the safety of the bakers or the well-being of the public, as clean and wholesome "bread does not depend upon whether the baker works but ten hours per day or only sixty hours a week."

Peckham indicated that limiting the work hours of bakers was not as serious a concern as limiting the working hours of miners, but there was yet another issue that factored into the Supreme Court's ruling in *Lochner*. That issue was the power of the State versus the liberty of individuals. Justice Peckham explained as much when he framed the case as being "a question of which of two powers or rights shall prevail—the power of the State to legislate or the right of the individual to liberty of person and freedom of contract." In this case, the right of individual liberty and freedom of contract prevailed.

In *Lochner*, Peckham declared that "the liberty of contract relating to labor includes both parties to it. The one has as much right to purchase as the other to sell labor." The rights are not equal, however. In a capitalist economy, the party contracting for the purchase of labor typically has a number of advantages over the party contracting to sell his or her labor. A most obvious advantage is that the employee relies on the income he or she receives from the employer. For this reason, the employer is in a better position to dictate the terms of employment to the employee.

Yet another advantage which employers enjoy is the at-will doctrine, which allows an employer to discharge an employee for any reason at all. The Supreme Court of Alabama in *Allied Supply Co. v. Brown*, 585 So. 2d 33, 35 (Ala.1991) described the doctrine as thus: "Employees at will can terminate their employment, or can be terminated by their employer, at any time, with or without cause or justification." The Supreme Court of Alabama noted that the "at-will" doctrine has been criticized as being harsh, but that it remained the law in Alabama. The Supreme Court of Tennessee held in *Payne v. Western & Atlantic. R.R.*, 81 Tenn. (1884) that men "must be left, without interference to buy and sell where they please, and to discharge or retain employees at will for good cause or for no cause, or even for bad cause without thereby being guilty of an unlawful act per se."

The Supreme Court of Tennessee in *Payne* quoted Judge Cooley, who stated: "It is a part of every man's civil rights that he be at liberty to refuse business relations with any person whomsoever, whether the refusal rests upon reason, or is the result of whim, caprice, prejudice or malice. With his reasons neither the public nor third persons have any legal concern." The logic expressed by Cooley here is precisely the type of logic used to defend racial segregation. Under such reasoning, it would be the civil right of every man to deny business relations to an African American solely on the basis of prejudice and it would not be of any legal concern to the African American who is denied business relations.

Should racists be forced to contract with African Americans? Holding such a view necessarily entails that certain rights on the part of the racist individual will be curtailed or infringed upon. How far then can the law go to establish racial equality? How far should the law go? These are questions that must be asked in order to assess the role that legislation has played in attempting to resolve the problem of racial discrimination in the United States. Prior to the civil rights movement, courts adopted the view that the law must not go too far in imposing against the segregationist because doing so would infringe on one's freedom to reject engaging in business relations with whomever one pleases and for whatever reason one chooses.

There is also the question of whether or not it is practical for racial problems to be addressed through imposing racial integration against the will of the racists. The argument against this is not only that it infringes upon the rights of the racist, but that it would perhaps be better for African Americans to avoid being around racists who harbor such negative, bigoted, and hateful views. Perhaps it may be in the best interests of African Americans to avoid such racist individuals altogether. The problem with this approach is that racial separation in of itself is not a solution to the problem so long as rules which are designed to restrict the rights of African Americans remain in place.

As a minister of the Nation of Islam, Malcolm X drew a distinction between segregation and racial separation. In an interview with Eleanor Fischer, Malcolm X explained his views, stating: "Segregation is that which is forced upon an inferior by a superior. Separation is done voluntarily by two equals." Segregation was imposed upon African Americans. Segregation was the law and this law was implemented to enforce racial inequality.

What of separation? Malcolm X said that separation was done on a voluntary basis by two equals. The problem here is that there was an unequal relationship and for this reason African Americans were not free to build separately or independently from the dominant white society. The Nation of Islam preached a doctrine of racial separation. To achieve this vision of separation, Elijah Muhammad advocated the creation of a separate state for black people. The Nation of Islam was free to preach separation, but the Nation of Islam lacked the power or capacity to truly carry out this separation and the American government was certainly not going to give in to the Nation of Islam's demands for land to build a separate nation. The Republic of New Afrika also demanded land to create a separate black nation.

Just as those who struggled for integration were met with a backlash, the Nation of Islam and other black separatist organizations were met with a similar backlash. Segregation was the law. Any attempts at racial integration were therefore a violation of that law, yet the segregationists did not view the black separatists as being preferable to the integrationists. On the contrary, black nationalism and the doctrine of black separation was viewed as a threat because it was an assertion of African American independence. The entire purpose of segregation was to keep African Americans in their place; to keep African Americans oppressed and subjugated. Integration was a threat to the status quo, but assertions of African American independence were also a threat as well because it was contrary to the goal of keeping African Americans subjugated.

Due to the threat of African American independence, building separate institutions from white people has been a challenge because when African Americans have done so it has been perceived as competing against white interests and eliminated for this reason. Ida B. Wells-Barnett was a well-known anti-lynching activist whose activism was motivated by the fact that her friend Thomas Moss had been lynched because Moss opened a grocery store, which was seen as a threat to a nearby white owned grocery store. African Americans did not have the freedom to patronize white owned businesses, but African Americans could not open and operate their own businesses without facing discrimination either. Therefore, separation alone is not a solution so long as African people do not have the necessary protection from white aggression.

Now that the matter of racial segregation has been briefly addressed, we shall return again to the manner in which the Supreme Court ruled on labor issues during the Lochner Era. In 1919, the Congress passed the Child Labor Law tax which imposed a tax on companies which employed child labor. A furniture manufacturer known as the Drexel Furniture Company incurred a ten percent tax on its net profits for allowing a fourteen year old boy to work in its factories. In *Bailey v. Drexel Furniture Co.*, 259 U.S. 20 (1922), the Supreme Court held that this tax imposed on Drexel was unconstitutional.

President William Taft, who was then serving as the Chief Justice of the Supreme Court, explained that the Child Labor Law "is attacked on the ground that it is a regulation of the employment of child labor in the states—an exclusively state function under the federal Constitution and within the reservations of the Tenth Amendment." The Tenth Amendment provides that: "The powers not delegated to the United States by the Constitution, nor prohibited by it to the States, are reserved to the States respectively, or to the people." In other words, since the Constitution did not delegate to the United States the ability to restrict child labor and because the use of child labor was not prohibited to any of the states, the argument which was made against the Child Labor Tax was that it was a violation of states' rights.

The Supreme Court in this case held that the tax was unconstitutional because the taxes were in fact a penalty against businesses which utilized child labor. Taft explained that "a court must be blind not to see that the so-called tax is imposed to stop the employment of children within the age limits prescribed. Its prohibitory and regulatory effect and purpose are palpable. All others can see and understand this. How can we properly shut our minds to it?"

In *Coppage v. Kansas*, 236 U.S. 1 (1915), the Supreme Court held that it was legal for an employer to forbid an employee from joining a union. The plaintiff, Coppage, was found to be guilty of violating a state statute. Section one of that statute provided: "That it shall be unlawful for any individual or member of any firm, or any agent, officer, or employee of any company or corporation to coerce, require, demand, or influence any person or persons to enter into any agreement, either written or verbal, not to join or become or remain a member of any labor organization or association as a condition of such person or persons securing employment or continuing in the employment of such individual, firm, or corporation."

The purpose of the law was to bar employers from preventing their employees from joining unions, which was precisely what Coppage did. Hedges was employed as a switchman by the St. Louis & San Francisco Railway Company. He was also a member of a labor organization called the Switchmen's Union of North America. Coppage was employed by the railway company as superintendent. Coppage requested Hedges to sign an agreement to withdraw from Switchmen's Union. Hedges was informed that if he did not sign it then he could not remain employed.

The Supreme Court held that the law enacted by the state of Kansas violated the "due process" clause of the Fourteenth Amendment. Justice Mahlon Pitney, who delivered the opinion, stated that "it is said by the Kansas Supreme Court (87 Kansas, p. 759) to be a matter of common knowledge that 'employees, as a rule, are not financially able to be as independent in making contracts for the sale of their labor as are employers in making contracts of purchase thereof.'" Of this inequality between employees and employers in making contracts, Justice Pitney remarked that "wherever the right of private property exists, there must and will be inequalities of fortune; and thus it naturally happens that parties negotiating about a contract are not equally unhampered by circumstances." Justice Pitney continued to explain that it is self-evident that "unless all things are held in common, some persons must have more property than others, it is from the nature of things impossible to uphold freedom of contract and the right of private property without at the same time recognizing as legitimate those inequalities of fortune that are the necessary result of the exercise of those rights."

Justice Pitney seemed to have been arguing that upholding freedom of contract and the right to private property cannot be done without also creating "inequalities of fortune", which are seen as the outcome of exercising such rights. Here one may ask whose freedom of contract and right to private property was the Supreme Court interested in protecting? If it would be a violation for a state to impose laws which bar employers from preventing employees from joining unions, would it not as equally be a violation of freedom of contract for employees to be barred from joining a union? The central issue being addressed by the Supreme Court was whether or not the freedom of contract of the employer should supersede that of the employee.

In the end, the Supreme Court held that it was not a significant infringement upon the right to freedom of contract of employees to allow employers to deny employees the ability to join a union. Justice Pitney explained that to "ask a man to agree, in advance, to refrain from affiliation with the union while retaining a certain position of employment, is not to ask him to give up any part of his constitutional freedom. He is free to decline the employment on those terms, just as the employer may decline to offer employment on any other; for 'It takes two to make a bargain.'" Justice Pitney continued to note that after having accepted employment under those terms, the employee is still free to join a union after the period of his employment ends.

An employee can, as Justice Pitney noted, either decline employment on those terms, which means trying to find employment elsewhere or the employee could merely join a union after the period of employment ends. The problem with such an approach is that if an employer is free to prevent employees from joining unions then the protections offered by the ability to unionize are nullified. There also is no guarantee that an employee will even find an employer who is willing to allow employees to join unions. The Supreme Court was effectively prioritizing the freedom of an employer to deny the right to unionize to its employees over the right of an employee to join a union.

Justice Oliver Holmes wrote a dissent to the Supreme Court's ruling in *Coppage*. Justice Holmes explained: "In present conditions a workman not unnaturally may believe that only by belonging to a union can he secure a contract that shall be fair to him. [...] If that belief, whether right or wrong, may be held by a reasonable man, it seems to me that it may be enforced by law in order to establish the equality of position between the parties in which liberty of contract begins."

Holmes concluded his dissent by writing: "I therefore think that the statute of Kansas, sustained by the Supreme Court of the State, did not go beyond a legitimate exercise of the police power, when it sought, not to require one man to employ another against his will, but to put limitations upon the sacrifice of rights which one man may exact from another as a condition of employment. Entertaining these views, I am constrained to dissent from the judgment in this case."

These rulings by the Supreme Court demonstrated the conflict between a laissez-faire approach which allows businesses to do as they please and the ability of the government to regulate businesses to avoid the harsher aspects of the capitalist system. These cases also demonstrated the tensions between protecting the rights of workers, while also protecting the right to freedom of contract of the employers. As was already noted, unrestrained capitalism can be very harsh for workers, who are given very little protection from exploitation. It is for this reason that states had to enact policies to protect workers through placing regulations on employers. Relying on the good-will of the employers was simply not enough, especially when the employers had a financial incentive to exploit workers.

Federal regulations and restrictions were especially required to protect African Americans, who not only required employee protections, but racial protections as well. This is also relevant to the point mentioned previously about African Americans being a legally created people. The rights offered to American citizens in the Constitution were not rights that were readily extended to African Americans. Instead, African Americans needed separate laws merely just to be recognized as citizens and to enjoy constitutional rights, such as liberty to contact.

After the aforementioned Lochner Era, the Supreme Court began to rule in favor of regulations and restrictions. The National Labor Relations Act of 1935 was passed to allow employees the ability to unionize without interference from the employer. This legislation was ruled to be constitutional by the Supreme Court in *National Labor Relations Board v. Jones & Laughlin Steel Corporation*, 301 U.S. 1 (1937). The Supreme Court held:

> That is a fundamental right. Employees have as clear a right to organize and select their representatives for lawful purposes as the respondent has to organize its business and select its own officers and agents. Discrimination and coercion to prevent the free exercise of the right of employees to self-organization and representation is a proper subject for condemnation by competent legislative authority. Long ago we stated the reason for labor organizations. We said that they were organized out of the necessities of the situation; that a single employee was helpless in dealing with an employer; that he was dependent ordinarily on his daily wage for the maintenance of himself and family; that if the employer refused to pay him the wages that he thought fair, he was nevertheless unable to leave the employ and resist arbitrary and unfair treatment; that union was essential to give laborers opportunity to deal on an equality with their employer.

In *West Coast Hotel Co. v. Parrish*, 300 U.S. 379 (1937), the Supreme Court ruled in favor of establishing a minimum wage for laborers. In this case, Elsie Parrish, who was employed as a chambermaid, brought a suit to recover the difference between the wages paid to her and the minimum wage fixed pursuant to the Washington state law, which set minimum wage at $14.50 per week of 48 hours. Chief Justice Charles Hughes explained:

> In each case the violation alleged by those attacking minimum wage regulation for women is deprivation of freedom of contract. What is this freedom? The Constitution does not speak of freedom of contract. It speaks of liberty and prohibits the deprivation of liberty without due process of law. In prohibiting that deprivation the Constitution does not recognize an absolute and uncontrollable liberty. Liberty in each of its phases has its history and connotation.

Chief Justice Hughes also explained that the "essential limitation of liberty in general governs freedom of contract in particular." Given that the liberty to contract is not absolute, the Supreme Court does have the ability to restrict freedom of contract. In this particular case, the Supreme Court decided that freedom of contract does not prevent states from enacting regulations to protect workers. Chief Justice Hughes mentions a number of regulations which had been implemented, such as an eight-hour work day for underground miners and smelters, forbidding the payment of seamen's wages in advance, and maintaining workmen's compensation laws. Chief Justice Hughes explained that "the legislature has necessarily a wide field of discretion in order that there may be suitable protection of health and safety, and that peace and good order may be promoted through regulations designed to insure wholesome conditions of work and freedom from oppression."

The Supreme Court was also concerned with protecting workers from undue economic exploitation because when workers are denied a living wage, it is taxpayers who are made to pay the cost of living for those workers:

> There is an additional and compelling consideration which recent economic experience has brought into a strong light. The exploitation of a class of workers who are in an unequal position with respect to bargaining power, and are thus relatively defenceless against the denial of a living wage, is not only detrimental to their health and wellbeing, but casts a direct burden for their support upon the community. What these workers lose in wages, the taxpayers are called upon to pay. The bare cost of living must be met.

The Supreme Court's ruling in *West Coast Hotel Co.* demonstrated that protecting workers meant limiting freedom of contract for employers. One of the fundamental principles in contract law is "freedom of contract." This refers to the freedom of persons to enter into contracts. It must be made clear that a contract is not merely an agreement between parties. A contract is a legally binding agreement and therefore the party which breaches the contract can be found to be legally liable for the breach. Contract law is based on the principle that one should be held accountable for the promises that one makes to others. Of course, not every promise is regarded by the courts as being a contract. Indeed, a contract refers to a very specific type of promise, consisting of three elements: an offer, acceptance, and consideration.

The Supreme Court held in *Dred Scott v. Sandford*, 60 U.S. (19 How.) 393 (1857) that Africans were not regarded as American citizens, regardless of if they were enslaved or freed. As such, the rights that were offered to American citizens were not enjoyed by African people. Enslaved Africans were regarded as chattel or property, which could be bought, sold, or traded. Freedom of contract meant the freedom to enter into contracts for the sale of enslaved persons. Owning an enslaved African was a property right for which the Constitution granted protection. Article IV, Section 2, Clause 3 of the Constitution reads:

No person held to service or labour in one state, under the laws thereof, escaping into another, shall, in consequence of any law or regulation therein, be discharged from such service or labor, but shall be delivered up on claim of the party to whom such service or labour may be due.

The word slave is not used in the clause, but the effect of the clause was obviously meant to ensure that slave masters had the right to have their property returned to them if that property were to escape. The right to private property protected the right of slave masters to own Africans. Much like other forms of property, banks were able to acquire a secured interest in slaves. Enslaved Africans were used as collateral for loans which were issued by banks and when borrowers defaulted on their loans, banks were able to take ownership over the slaves.

The struggles that African Americans continued to endure after the abolition of slavery was in many ways a struggle for freedom of contract. The racial segregation which followed the abolition of slavery was aimed at restricting the ability of African Americans to exercise freedom of contract. This struggle was clearly illustrated in *Civil Rights Cases*, 109 U.S. 3 (1883), which were cases that were brought before the Supreme Court regarding the first and second sections of a civil rights act which was passed by Congress on March 1, 1875, entitled "An Act to protect all citizens in their civil and legal rights."

The plaintiffs, in five cases from lower courts, were bringing suits alleging civil rights violations. The claims included denying to persons of color the accommodations and privileges of an inn and denying to individuals the privileges and accommodations of a theatre, along with other claims. In delivering the opinion of the Supreme Court, Justice Joseph Bradley explained: "The essence of the law is, not to declare broadly that all persons shall be entitled to the full and equal enjoyment of the accommodations, advantages, facilities, and privileges of inns, public conveyances, and theaters; but that such enjoyment shall not be subject to any conditions applicable only to citizens of a particular race or color, or who had been in a previous condition of servitude."

A Legally Created People

Congress' power to enact civil rights legislation rests in the Fourteenth Amendment, which stipulates that "no State shall make or enforce any law which shall abridge the privileges or immunities of citizens of the United States; nor shall any State deprive any person of life, liberty, or property without due process of law; nor deny to any person within its jurisdiction the equal protection of the laws." Justice Bradley explained that there was no question that the Fourteenth Amendment "nullifies and makes void all State legislation, and State action of every kind, which impairs the privileges and immunities of citizens of the United States, or which injures them in life, liberty, or property without due process of law, or which denies to any of them the equal protection of the laws."

Bradley explained that the Fourteenth Amendment "does not invest Congress with power to legislate upon subjects which are within the domain of State legislation; but to provide modes of relief against State legislation, or State action, of the kind referred to." Justice Bradley continued to explain that the Fourteenth Amendment "does not authorize Congress to create a code of municipal law for the regulation of private rights, but to provide modes of redress against the operation of State laws, and the action of State officers, executive or judicial, when these are subversive of the fundamental rights specified in the amendment." Bradley concluded that "until some State law has been passed, or some State action through its officers or agents has been taken, adverse to the rights of citizens sought to be protected by the Fourteenth Amendment, no legislation of the United States under said amendment, nor any proceeding under such legislation, can be called into activity: for the prohibitions of the amendment are against State laws and acts done under State authority."

In *Civil Rights Cases*, the Supreme Court, in essence, held that private citizens have the right to engage in racial segregation and that the Fourteenth Amendment does not authorize Congress to regulate the actions of private citizens who choose to discriminate on the basis of race. The problem with such an interpretation is that it severely limited the enforcement of the Fourteenth Amendment by allowing individuals to discriminate. More so than this, however, the Supreme Court ruling held that individuals could deny African Americans the freedom to contract. This will be addressed in more detail, but the point to be made here is that the Supreme Court ruling in *Civil Right Cases* undermined important pieces of legislation which were intended to ensure that African Americans were protected from discrimination, as well as given equal treatment and opportunities under the law.

Yet another problem that arises from interpreting the Fourteenth Amendment is what constitutes due process? This is important because the Fourteenth Amendment provides, as previously noted, that no "State shall make or enforce any law which shall abridge the privileges or immunities of citizens of the United States; nor shall any State deprive any person of life, liberty, or property, without due process of law; nor deny to any person within its jurisdiction the equal protection of the laws." The Fourteenth

Amendment protects citizens against the arbitrary deprivation of rights and privileges, but what happens when the deprivation of such rights and privileges are written into the law and upheld by the courts? At this point the citizen is no longer being deprived of any rights without due process because the law itself enforces such deprivation of those rights.

In *Plessy v. Ferguson*, 163 U.S. 537 (1896), the Supreme Court stated, "we think the enforced separation of the races, as applied to the internal commerce of the State, neither abridges the privileges or immunities of the colored man, deprives him of his property without due process of law, nor denies him the equal protection of the laws, within the meaning of the Fourteenth Amendment [...]." The Supreme Court here was willing to permit racial segregation, stating that enforced separation of the races was not depriving an individual of the right of due process.

The laws were not so straightforward as to outright ban African Americans from voting because of their racial identity. Instead, the voting restrictions appeared to be racially neutral on their face. This included policies such as a poll tax, which required voters to pay a tax in order to register to vote. On its face a poll tax appears racially neutral. In fact, poll taxes have historically barred white citizens from voting just as it has barred black citizens, but the "grandfather clause" was one of the means by which white citizens could escape the requirement of a poll tax. The grandfather clause exempted individuals who were able to vote prior to January 1, 1867, or individuals who were the son or grandson of an individual who could vote prior to that time. Prior to 1867, African Americans were not eligible to vote in Louisiana and for this reason the grandfather clause would not apply.

In *Louisiana v. United States*, 380 U.S. 145 (1965), the Supreme Court held that Louisiana's voter restriction policies were unconstitutional. In 1921, Louisiana replaced the grandfather clause with an "interpretation test" which required an applicant for registration to "give a reasonable interpretation" of any clause in Louisiana's Constitution or the Constitution of the United States. From the adoption of the 1921 interpretation test until 1944, African Americans never exceeded one percent of the registered voting population. Prior to 1944, African Americans only had a slight interest in voting since Louisiana's laws prevented African Americans from voting in the Democratic Party primary election. Justice Hugo Black, who delivered the opinion of the Court, noted that the Supreme Court had previously invalidated an identical primary law in Texas in *Smith v. Allwright*, 321 U.S. 649 (1944).

Black noted that the white primary system had so effectively barred African Americans from voting that the "interpretation test" as a device for disenfranchisement was ignored. Due to an increase in the number of registered African American voters and the 1954 Supreme Court decision which invalidated the laws upholding school segregation, Louisiana sought new ways to bar African Americans from voting. A "Segregation Committee" was created by the Louisiana Legislature for this

A Legally Created People

purpose.

In *Herman v. Forssenius*, 380 U.S. 528 (1965), the Supreme Court held that Virginia's voter registration policies were unconstitutional. Virginia eliminated the poll tax requirement for federal elections and substituted a provision in which the federal voter could qualify either by paying the customary poll tax or by filing a certificate of residence six months before the election. The Supreme Court held that these new restrictions which were implemented by Virginia were in violation of the Twenty-fourth Amendment.

The poll tax in Virginia was implemented for the purpose of preventing African Americans from being able to vote. There was no secret about this at all. At the Virginia Constitutional Convention of 1902, the sponsor of the suffrage plan in which the poll tax was included, stated very frankly: "Discrimination! Why, that is precisely what we propose; that, exactly, is what this Convention was elected for—to discriminate to the very extremity of permissible action under the limitations of the Federal Constitution, with a view to the elimination of every negro voter who can be gotten rid of, legally, without materially impairing the numerical strength of the white electorate." This statement, which was delivered by Carter Glass, is very revealing not only because it demonstrated that there was no pretense about denying African Americans the ability to vote, but also because it demonstrated that racist legislators were trying to discriminate as much as they could within the limits of the Constitution.

In *Harper v. Virginia Board of Elections*, 383

U.S. 663 (1966), the Supreme Court overturned the prior ruling in *Breedlove v. Suttles*, 302 U.S. 277 (1937) holding that poll taxes violated the Equal Protection Clause of the Fourteenth Amendment and were therefore unconstitutional. In his dissent, Justice Hugo Black wrote that the Court's decision was "to no extent based on a finding that the Virginia law as written or as applied is being used as a device or mechanism to deny Negro citizens of Virginia the right to vote on account of their color." Black explained that if "the record could support a finding that the law as written or applied has such an effect, the law would of course be unconstitutional as a violation of the Fourteenth and Fifteenth Amendments and also 42 U. S. C. § 1971 (a)." Black appeared to disagree with the Court's ruling "that the Equal Protection Clause necessarily bars all States from making payment of a state tax, any tax, a prerequisite to voting." In Black's view *Breedlove* was correctly decided because the "mere fact that a law results in treating some groups differently from others does not, of course, automatically amount to a violation of the Equal Protection Clause."

The Voting Rights Act of 1965 was passed to enforce the voting rights provisions of the Fifteenth Amendment. The second section of the Fifteenth Amendment gave Congress the power to enforce the Fifteenth Amendment through passing the appropriate legislation, although it took pressure from the civil rights movement for Congress to finally pass legislation to protect the voting rights of African Americans. Merely just being citizens should have guaranteed African Americans equal voting rights under the law, but this was not the case. The very purpose for implementing the Fifteenth Amendment was to protect the voting rights of African Americans, but even then, additional legislation was needed to protect those voting rights.

Justice Harlan's dissent in *Civil Rights Cases* helped to highlight how selective the Supreme Court has been with which rights it has chosen to enforce. Harlan stated that "the substance and spirit of the recent amendments of the Constitution have been sacrificed by a subtle and ingenious verbal criticism." Harlan also explained "that the court has departed from the familiar rule requiring, in the interpretation of constitutional provisions, that full, effect be given to the intent with which they were adopted." Harlan continued to explain: "The purpose of the first section of the act of Congress of March 1, 1875, was to prevent *race* discrimination in respect of the accommodations and facilities of inns, public conveyances, and places of public amusement."

Justice Harlan took issue with the fact that the Supreme Court's ruling in the case was contrary to the intent with which the Fourteenth Amendment was adopted. Justice Harlan explained that section 2, article IV of the Constitution gave Congress the authority to pass the Fugitive Slave Law of 1793, which established "a mode for the recovery of fugitive slaves, and prescribing a penalty against any person who should knowingly and willingly obstruct or hinder the master, his agent, or attorney, in seizing, arresting, and recovering the fugitive, or who should rescue the fugitive from him, or who should harbor or conceal the slave after notice that he was a fugitive."

Justice Harlan's reference to the Fugitive Slave clause of the Constitution is noteworthy here because it demonstrated that the Supreme Court was willing to uphold the right of slave masters to retain control over their slaves, but the Supreme Court was much less willing to enforce constitutional measures which were designed to prevent racial discrimination. Justice Harlan noted that "the Constitution recognized the master's right of property in his fugitive slave, and, as incidental thereto, the right of seizing and recovering him, regardless of any State law, or regulation, or local custom whatsoever" and that "the right of the master to have his slave, thus escaping, delivered up on claim, being guaranteed by the Constitution, the fair implication was that the national government was clothed with appropriate authority and functions to enforce it."

Justice Harlan noted that the constitutionality of the Fugitive Slave Act of 1850, much like the Fugitive Slave Law of 1973, rested "solely upon the implied power of Congress to enforce the master's rights." Harlan continues to note that these provisions "placed at the disposal of the master seeking to recover his fugitive slave, substantially the whole power of the nation." Justice Harlan's dissent rightfully pointed out that the American judicial system found no problem with enforcing constitutional provisions which protected the right of a slave master to maintain enslaved persons as property. Fugitive slave provisions were meant to ensure that individuals who no longer wished to be enslaved had no say in the matter. Such individuals were forcibly returned if they ran away. When it came to the Fourteenth Amendment, there was much less willingness on the part of the judicial system to enforce the protections which the Constitution offered to African Americans. Fugitive slave provisions benefited slave masters, even if doing so was against the desire of the enslaved. Similarly, the Supreme Court's willingness to uphold segregation benefited racist segregationists, against the desires of those who were excluded because of these segregationist policies.

The willingness to enforce the Fugitive Slave Clause in the Constitution was demonstrated in *Prigg v. Pennsylvania*, 41 U.S. (16 Pet.) 539 (1842), which was another Supreme Court case. Edward Prigg was a citizen of Maryland who was indicted in Pennsylvania for kidnapping Margaret Morgan, an African woman who was born into slavery and escaped to Pennsylvania. Under the laws of Maryland, Morgan was a slave for life to her master, Margaret Ashmore. Prigg tracked down and captured Morgan in Pennsylvania for the purpose of returning Morgan into slavery.

By the time of this case Pennsylvania had already abolished slavery. The act which outlawed slavery stated: "All persons, as well negroes and mulattoes, as others, who shall be born within this state, shall not be deemed and considered as servants for life or slaves; and all servitude for life, or slavery of children, in consequence of slavery of their mothers, in the case of all children born within this state, from and after the passing of this act as aforesaid, shall be and hereby is utterly taken away, extinguished and for ever abolished."

The Pennsylvania law which Prigg was charged with violating stated:

> If any person or persons shall, from and after the passing of this act, by force and violence, take and carry away, or cause to be taken or carried away, and shall, by fraud or false pretense, seduce, or cause to be seduced, or shall attempt so to take, carry away or seduce, any negro or mulatto, from any part or parts of this commonwealth, to any other place or places whatsoever, out of this common-wealth, with a design and intention of selling and disposing of, or of causing to be sold, or of keeping and detaining, or of causing to be kept and detained, such negro or mulatto, as a slave or servant for life, or for any term whatsoever, every such person or persons, his or their aiders or abettors, shall on conviction thereof, in any court of this commonwealth having competent jurisdiction, be deemed guilty of a felony, and shall forfeit and pay, at the discretion of the court passing the sentence, a sum not less than five hundred, nor more than one thousand dollars, one-half whereof shall be paid to the person or persons who shall prosecute for the same, and the other half to this commonwealth; and moreover, shall be sentenced to undergo a servitude for any term or terms not less than seven years, nor exceeding twenty-one years, and shall be confined and kept to hard labor, fed and clothed in the manner as is directed by the penal laws of this commonwealth for

persons convicted of robbery.

The Supreme Court ultimately reversed the conviction of Prigg, holding that "under and in virtue of the Constitution, the owner of a slave is clothed with entire authority, in every state in the Union, to seize and recapture his slave, whenever he can do it without any breach of the peace, or any illegal violence." The Supreme Court concluded that the act of "Pennsylvania upon which this indictment is founded, is unconstitutional and void. It purports to punish as a public offence against that state, the very act of seizing and removing a slave by his master, which the Constitution of the United States was designed to justify and uphold."

Another issue raised in Harlan's dissent in *Civil Rights Cases* is whether or not inns can legally exclude individuals. Harlan quotes Justice Coleridge, who explained: "The innkeeper is not to select his guests. He has no right to say to one. you shall come to my inn, and to another you shall not, as every one coming and conducting himself in a proper manner has a right to be received; and for this purpose innkeepers are a sort of public servants, they having in return a kind of privilege of entertaining travellers and supplying them with what they want." Based on this, Harlan concluded that the public nature of an innkeeper's employment "forbids him from discriminating against any person asking admission as a guest on account of the race or color of that person."

The ruling in *Civil Rights Cases* was indicative of the fact that although legislation had been put in place to protect African Americans from racial discrimination, the Supreme Court tended to narrowly interpret these policies. As has been previously demonstrated, the justification for doing so was that a broad interpretation of such legislation would violate the rights of private citizens, who have the right to exclude people on the basis of race. The Supreme Court in *Civil Rights Cases* interpreted the Fourteenth Amendment to apply to State acts, as opposed to the acts of private citizens.

The maintenance of segregated facilities was justified by the "separate but equal" doctrine put forward by the Supreme Court in *Plessy*. This doctrine was successfully challenged in *Brown v. Board of Education of Topeka*, 347 U.S. 483 (1954), in which the Supreme Court held that the separate but equal doctrine could not apply to public schools because "[s]eparate educational facilities are inherently unequal." The Supreme Court further held "that the plaintiffs and others similarly situated for whom the actions have been brought are, by reason of the segregation complained of, deprived of the equal protection of the laws guaranteed by the Fourteenth Amendment."

Apart from the argument to be made about the equal quality of facilities which was addressed in *Brown*, there is also the question of equality of liberty. All American citizens should have the same protections and the same rights under the law. This should mean that public facilities which are open to white people should be just as much open and available to African Americans. Unfortunately, even after the Fourteenth Amendment granted African

Americans citizenship, citizenship did not mean equality under the law. In *Brown*, the Supreme Court finally decided to hold that segregation was a violation of the Constitution.

The ruling in *Brown* was a blow against segregation, but it was also a blow to black educators as well. Bobby E. Wright explained that "as a result of the 'infamous' 1954 school desegregation decision, Blacks have lost an estimated 35,000 teaching and administrative positions in the South. Former Black principals of Black schools are now janitors in integrated schools and the same thing is going to happen to Black teachers in the North."

There is also the matter of freedom of contract, which was discussed previously in the context of employment. The Supreme Court wrestled with where to draw the limit to the freedom of contract in the context of employment. The Supreme Court was in the position of trying to balance the necessity of protecting workers, while also preserving the liberties of employers. This balance becomes even more complicated when one introduces the variable of race. Not only is there a question of protecting the workers while minimally intruding upon the rights of employers, but also the question of protecting African American workers from racial discrimination, given that at one point freedom of contract also meant freedom to discriminate on the basis of race.

Freedom of contract meant that a white employer had the freedom to deny an African American solely on the basis of race. This meant the denial of things such as employment, rent, or, denial of service, to give but a few examples. This was perfectly legal under American law prior to the abolition of slavery. There were no provisions which guarded against racial discrimination in the process of contract formation and African Americans were not regarded as being citizens. African Americans were regarded as property and, as already noted, freedom of contract meant the freedom to buy and sell that property; the freedom to buy and sell Africans. Africans were the subject of contracts but did not have any legally protected rights to freely engage in contracts for their own benefit.

The Civil Rights Act of 1866, which was passed after the abolition of slavery, finally addressed the problem regarding the lack of protection for African Americans in regard to making contracts. The 1866 act not only made African people citizens under American law, but it provided freedom of contract to all citizens. Section 1981 of the 1866 Civil Rights Act provides:

All persons within the jurisdiction of the United States shall have the same right in every State and Territory to make and enforce contracts, to sue, be parties, give evidence, and to the full and equal benefit of all laws and proceedings for the security of persons and property as is enjoyed by white citizens, and shall be subject to like punishment, pains, penalties, taxes, licenses, and exactions of every kind, and to no other.

In theory, African Americans were just as free as white citizens to make and enforce contracts, but in practice there was still no equality. This is demonstrated by Jim Crow laws, which barred African Americans from accessing the same facilities as white people. This also included housing and employment discrimination, which adversely impacted the ability of African Americans to find shelter and to earn a living. This was the very thing which the Civil Rights Act of 1866 was meant to prevent. but, as was typically the case with legislation that was meant to prevent racial discrimination, the Supreme Court applied a very narrow view regarding when such protections against racial discrimination applied.

Patterson v. McLean Credit Union, 491 U.S. 164 (1989) offers an example of the Supreme Court's very narrow approach to interpreting the protections offered by § 1981. Brenda Patterson, an African American woman, was employed by McLean Credit Union as a teller and a file coordinator. After being laid off in 1982, Patterson commenced a suit against her former employer. She alleged that Mclean Credit Union, in violation of 14 Stat. 27, 42 U.S.C. § 1981, had harassed her, failed to promote her to an intermediate accounting clerk position, and then discharged her because of her race. Patterson also claimed this conduct amounted to an intentional infliction of emotional distress, actionable under North Carolina tort law. The District Court determined that a claim for racial harassment is not actionable under § 1981 and declined to submit that part of the case to the jury.

The Supreme Court held that Patterson did not have a claim under § 1981, given that the scope of this statute prohibited the "mak[ing] and enforce[ment]" of contracts alone. Based on the language of § 1981, Justice Anthony Kennedy explained: "Where an alleged act of discrimination does not involve the impairment of one of these specific rights, § 1981 provides no relief. Section 1981 cannot be construed as a general proscription of racial discrimination in all aspects of contract relations, for it expressly prohibits discrimination only in the making and enforcement of contracts." The Supreme Court ultimately held that Patterson's claim was not actionable under § 1981 because the conduct which she alleged was not related to the formation of the contract.

Peterson alleged that she was subjected to various forms of racial harassment from her supervisor. This included being periodically stared at for several minutes at a time; being given too many tasks, which led to her complaining that she was under too much pressure; the tasks that she was given were sweeping and dusting tasks which were not given to white employees; and she also alleged that she was passed over for promotion. Justice Kennedy explained that with "the exception perhaps of her claim that respondent refused to promote her to a position as an accountant [...] none of the conduct which petitioner alleges as part of the racial harassment against her involves either a refusal to make a contract with her or the impairment of her ability to enforce her established contract rights." Justice Kennedy also explained: "Interpreting § 1981 to cover post-formation conduct unrelated to an employee's right to enforce his or her contract, such as incidents relating to the conditions of employment, is not only inconsistent with that statute's limitation to the making and enforcement of contracts, but would also undermine the detailed and well crafted procedures for conciliation and resolution of Title VII claims."

The Supreme Court's ruling in *Patterson v. McLean Credit Union* held that § 1981 does not apply to discrimination which occurs after the contract has been formed. In other words, § 1981 ensures that African Americans have the freedom to enter into employment contracts, but are not protected from being discriminated against after being employed. Based on this interpretation, § 1981 does not offer unlimited protection against racial discrimination and employers are free to discriminate, just so long as they do so after the contract has been formed, at least where § 1981 is concerned. The other statute which provides protection against employment discrimination is Title VII.

The passage of the Civil Rights Act of 1964 was a landmark moment in the civil rights movement and one of the provisions of this act was Title VII. Title VII of the Civil Rights Act of 1964 prohibits employers from discriminating against employees on the basis of race, color, religion, sex or national origin. Since the passage of the Civil Rights Act of 1964, the Supreme Court has, on more than one occasion, ruled in ways which would make it more difficult for employees to prevail under Title VII or Title VII related claims. One example of this was the ruling in *Price Waterhouse v. Hopkins*, 490 U.S. 228 (1989). Ann Hopkins brought a lawsuit against her employer, Price Waterhouse, alleging sex discrimination pursuant to Title VII. Hopkins was the only female candidate proposed for partnership in 1982 out of the eighty-eight persons proposed for partnership. She was denied the partnership and alleged that she was discriminated against on the basis of her sex.

The partners in Hopkins' office praised her character as well as her accomplishments, but Hopkins was also known for her abrasive behavior. Hopkins' poor interpersonal skills ultimately doomed her bid for partnership. Despite her professional success and strong qualities, Hopkins was described as being "sometimes overly aggressive, unduly harsh, difficult to work with, and impatient with staff."

The Supreme Court noted that there was evidence to demonstrate that some partners reacted strongly to Hopkins' behavior because she was a woman. She was described as being "macho" and another partner suggested that she "overcompensated for being a woman". Several partners criticized her use of profanity. One partner suggested that those partners objected to her swearing only "because it's a lady using foul language." Hopkins was told that if she wanted to improve her chances she had to "walk more femininely, talk more femininely, dress more femininely, wear make-up, have her hair styled, and wear jewelry."

Based on the facts of the case, Price Waterhouse did have legitimate concerns about Hopkins' interpersonal skills, which were assessed when determining whether or not to make her a partner.

Yet, much of the negative response to Hopkins' behavior was based on sex stereotyping. The problem was not merely Hopkins' behavior, but that the partners believed that it was improper for a woman to behave in the manner that she was behaving. For this reason, one of the questions addressed by the Supreme Court in this case was whether or not Hopkins could still prevail on her sexual discrimination claim, despite the fact that Price Waterhouse articulated a legitimate reason for why Hopkins was denied partnership.

The Supreme Court looked at the language of Title VII, which prohibited an employer from making an adverse decision against an employee "because of such individual's . . . sex." The Supreme Court concluded that the phrase "because of" in Title VII meant "but-for causation." Justice Brennan concluded that in "determining whether a particular factor was a but-for cause of a given event, we begin by assuming that that factor was present at the time of the event, and then ask whether, even if that factor had been absent, the event nevertheless would have transpired in the same way."

This ruling meant that a defendant could escape liability if the defendant is able to prove that but for the alleged discrimination, the plaintiff would not have suffered an adverse employment action—examples of an adverse employment action include being discharged, demoted, or denied for a position. Brennan explained that "once a plaintiff in a Title VII case shows that gender played a motivating part in an employment decision, the defendant may avoid a finding of liability only by proving that it would have made the same decision even if it had not allowed gender to play such a role." In *Price Waterhouse*, the defendant merely needed to demonstrate that Hopkins would have still been denied for partnership even if her gender did not play a motivating factor. The ruling in *Price Waterhouse* allowed defendants to escape liability through proving that a legitimate reason motivated the employment decision, even if race, gender, religion, or other classes protected under Title VII were taken into consideration as well, while also imposing a higher standard for plaintiffs to meet in order to prevail in Title VII cases. Though *Price Waterhouse* was a gender discrimination case, the ruling also applied to racial discrimination cases under Title VII as well.

Congress passed the Civil Rights Act of 1991, which overturned the Supreme Court's narrow interpretation of Title VII in *Price Waterhouse*. Section 107(a) of the 1991 Civil Rights Act Amendment provides that an "unlawful employment practice is established when the complaining party demonstrates that race, color, religion, sex, or national origin was a motivating factor for any employment practice, even though other factors motivated the practice."

The 1991 civil rights bill made it easier for plaintiffs to prevail in Title VII discrimination cases by overturning the "but-for" requirement which the Supreme Court imposed in *Price Waterhouse*. The Supreme Court ruled, however, that a but-for causation analysis applied to retaliation cases, even if such cases arose out of an alleged violation of Title VII. The Supreme Court made this ruling in

University of Texas Southwestern Medical Center v. Nassar, 570 U.S. 338 (2013).

Dr. Naiel Nassar, a physician of Middle Eastern descent who was both a University faculty member and a hospital staff physician, claimed that Dr. Levine, one of his supervisors at the University, was biased against him on account of his religion and ethnic heritage. Nassar complained to Dr. Fitz, Levine's supervisor, but after he arranged to continue working at the hospital without also being on the University's faculty, he resigned from his teaching post and sent a letter to Fitz and others, stating that he was leaving because of Dr. Levine's harassment.

Nassar filed a suit alleging Title VII violations. The first claim was a status-based discrimination claim under §2000e–2(a), claiming that Dr. Levine's racially and religiously motivated harassment resulted in his constructive discharge from the University. The second claim was that Dr. Fitz's effort to prevent the hospital from hiring him was in retaliation for complaining about Dr. Levine's harassment, in violation of §2000e–3(a).

Regarding Nassar's retaliation claim, the Supreme Court addressed the question of whether or not the lessened causation standard applied by Congress' statutory amendment to the Civil Rights Act of 1964 applied to retaliation claims. Justice Anthony Kennedy stated of the new standard imposed by Congress' 1991 act: "An employee who alleges status-based discrimination under Title VII need not show that the causal link between injury and wrong is so close that the injury would not have occurred but for the act. So-called but-for causation is not the test. It suffices instead to show that the motive to discriminate was one of the employer's motives, even if the employer also had other, lawful motives that were causative in the employer's decision." Justice Kennedy explained that prior to *Nassar*, the Supreme Court had not addressed the question of the causation showing required to establish liability for a Title VII retaliation claim. For this reason, the Supreme Court relied on its prior ruling in *Gross v. FBL Financial Services, Inc.*, 557 U.S. 167 (2009).

In *Gross*, the Supreme Court held that the Age Discrimination in Employment Act of 1967 (ADEA) required that the plaintiff prove that the plaintiff's age was the but-for cause of the prohibited conduct, much like the standard set by the Supreme Court in *Price Waterhouse*. The ADEA provides that "'[i]t shall be unlawful for an employer . . . to fail or refuse to hire or to discharge any individual or otherwise discriminate against any individual with respect to his compensation, terms, conditions, or privileges of employment, because of such individual's age.'" The Supreme Court held that the "because of" phrase in the ADEA meant that a but-for standard applied to the ADEA. Therefore, for a plaintiff to prevail in an ADEA claim, the plaintiff must demonstrate but for the plaintiff's age, the defendant would have not engaged in the adverse employment action. This also means that a defendant can escape liability by demonstrating that there was a non-discriminatory, legitimate reason for why the action was taken.

The Supreme Court noted that the ruling in *Gross* was instructive in the case of *Nassar*. Moreover,

Justice Kennedy noted that "Title VII's antiretaliation provision, which is set forth in §2000e–3(a), appears in a different section from Title VII's ban on status-based discrimination." For this reason, the Supreme Court did not apply the 1991 act by Congress. Title VII's retaliation provision provides: "It shall be an unlawful employment practice for an employer to discriminate against any of his employees . . . because he has opposed any practice made an unlawful employment practice by this subchapter, or because he has made a charge, testified, assisted, or participated in any manner in an investigation, proceeding, or hearing under this subchapter."

The Supreme Court applied a "but-for" causation standard to Title VII's retaliation provision. This meant that although employment discrimination claims which arose under Title VII no longer required a "but-for" standard, if an employer were to retaliate against an employee for complaining about discrimination, the employee would have to meet the "but-for" standard set by the Supreme Court. As explained before, the Supreme Court applies the "but-for" standard due to the language of Title VII, but this interpretation of the language of Title VII is one which frustrates the very goal which Title VII was meant to accomplish.

For African people, becoming equal citizens and enjoying the rights which are guaranteed to an American citizen under the Constitution required an extensive overhaul of America's laws, but even then struggles persisted as many of these laws were not strictly enforced and it, as has been demonstrated, the

Supreme Court often interpreted these laws in such a manner as to diminish the ability of these laws to protect African Americans from the very racial discrimination which the laws were designed to prohibit. Wright referred to African Americans as a legally created people because of the fact that legislation had to be implemented in order for African Americans to become citizens, but even with this legislation in place, the legal rights of African Americans continue to be held in a very precarious balance.